Starting Up

For ~~Lieut Mary~~

Small payback for all
the love respect and
appreciation you've sent
my way over the years.

Love,
Mark.

Starting Up

CRITICAL LESSONS
FROM 10 NEW SCHOOLS

EDITED BY

Lisa Arrastía
Marvin Hoffman

FOREWORD BY

Pedro Noguera

Teachers College
Columbia University
New York and London

Published by Teachers College Press, 1234 Amsterdam Avenue,
New York, NY 10027

Library of Congress Cataloging-in-Publication Data

Starting up : critical lessons from 10 new schools / edited by Lisa Arrastia,
Marvin Hoffman ; foreword by Pedro Noguera.
   p. cm.
  Includes bibliographical references and index.
  ISBN 978-0-8077-5307-1 (pbk. : alk. paper)
  ISBN 978-0-8077-5308-8 (hardcover : alk. paper)
   1. Urban schools—United States—Case studies. 2. New Schools—United
States—Case studies. 3. Charter schools—United States—Case studies.
4. School improvement programs—United States—Case studies. I. Arrastia, Lisa.
II. Hoffman, Marvin, 1939–
  LC5131.S67 2012
  370.9173'2—dc23

                                                                2011051425

ISBN 978-0-8077-5307-1 (paperback)
ISBN 978-0-8077-5308-8 (hardcover)

Printed on acid-free paper

Manufactured in the United States of America

19 18 17 16 15 14 13 12   8 7 6 5 4 3 2 1

Most of us realize that, only when we envisage a better social order, do we find the present one in many ways unendurable and stir ourselves to repair. The sight and description of the new schools at the present time ... make it uniquely possible to identify what is wrong with the traditional schools.

—Maxine Greene, *Teaching as Possibility*

Contents

Creating New Schools in These New Times

In most American cities, public schools are indispensable institutions that are of vital importance to the health and well-being, hope and aspirations of the communities they serve. They provide the recreation areas where big children play ball, small children play on swings and slides, and others walk their dogs. They provide meeting spaces where community groups convene, often at no charge. On Election Day, they serve as polling places where residents cast their votes, and during times of crisis—earthquakes, hurricanes, and terrorist attacks—they serve as sites of refuge and provide temporary shelter (Stone et al., 2001).

As state institutions with a relatively stable source of funding, public schools operate with a high degree of reliability and predictability. They have water and heat (sometimes even air conditioning), and for nearly half the year they provide children with adult supervision. They are centers of employment for teachers, administrators, custodians, security guards, and cafeteria workers. They provide children with meals (sometimes breakfast and lunch), a warm place to be when it's cold, and even limited access to a school nurse. In economically depressed, socially isolated neighborhoods where there are no banks, supermarkets, or pharmacies, public schools are almost always present, and typically they serve all of the children who live nearby. This includes the children of the homeless, the children of the incarcerated and infirm, the documented and the undocumented immigrants who speak no English and who are unfamiliar with the customs of the new land they call home.

No other institution in American society is as open and accessible to the children of the poor and no institution is as scrutinized or as frequently castigated. In part, this is because while they may be stable and accessible, too often urban public schools are consistent at the wrong things: consistently ineffective at educating children, the primary function for which they were created, and consistent at failing to meet the needs and aspirations of the parents they serve. This is why a growing number of parents in America's cities are clamoring for access to new schools, many of which are charter schools. They are frustrated and fed up with the indifference and incompetence they too frequently encounter in traditional public schools, and they are ready to embrace something new, even when the schools that open up are untested and not as democratic with respect to rules and procedures as the schools they've known.

The movie *Waiting for Superman* may have been wrong on many issues—about blaming teacher unions for all of the problems that beset public education, about not acknowledging the effects of poverty on school access and school performance, and about uncritically claiming that charter schools are better than public schools—but it was right about one thing for sure: Public schools are in danger of losing their most reliable constituents. This is even true for the ones sociologist William Julius Wilson described as the "truly disadvantaged" (1987). For the parents of America's most disadvantaged children, public schools are often not the beacon of hope or the pathway to a better life that they so desperately need. They know from their own experiences that school failure is normalized in many inner-city schools, that dropping out is accepted as a form of collateral damage in an educational system based on triage, and that many of the adults are far more concerned about their employment interests than the education of the children they serve. They also know that the educators who serve their children and work in their schools are like other middle-class families elsewhere and would never place their own children in the schools where they work.

Despite these failings, public schools are paradoxically both vital to the economic and social infrastructure of the communities they serve, and the source of many of the problems confronting those communities. Several studies of urban public schools have found that they are often implicated in the problems confronting the people who reside in America's poorest cities, and in some cases they exacerbate them.[1] Instead of being responsive to the needs of children and their parents, they are often overwhelmed by them and rendered ineffectual because they lack resources and the capacity to respond. When one fully grasps the enormity of the obstacles they face— children who lack supportive families, who arrive at school hungry and sick, who have never attended preschool and have been exposed to abuse and violence—it is easy to understand why they are so frequently overwhelmed. Throughout America, the neediest children arrive at school with a variety of social and emotional challenges, and more often than not, they are sent to schools that are under-resourced and floundering.

It is an absolute setup. Under the guise of equity, we now hold schools that serve children in impoverished communities to the same standards as schools in more affluent areas. Not surprisingly, schools that serve children who have all of their material needs met and that receive considerably more public dollars generally perform at a higher academic level. In contrast, in the most marginalized neighborhoods where gangs control the streets and drug trafficking is the primary source of income for many residents, these social forces also show up within schools. Schools are not fortresses and they do not exist in a vacuum. More often than not, the social, economic, and political influences that are pervasive within a neighborhood show up within a school. Our public schools reflect our strengths and weaknesses as a society, and in urban areas where poverty is concentrated and racial segregation is the norm, we get the schools our inequity and neglect provide.

We also suffer the consequences. When hopelessness and despair flourish within a community, we should not be surprised when they also seep into the fabric and structure of schools. I have witnessed this symbiotic relationship between school and community on numerous occasions. Once, when visiting Mount Vernon High School in Mount Vernon, New York, I was struck by the names and photographs of individuals who appeared on the walls of the corridors of the school: doctors, judges, actors, clergy, entertainers, and professional athletes. I asked the administrator who was taking me on the tour whether or not the school was still capable of producing such a distinguished group of graduates. He shook his head and explained: "Times have changed. We don't get young people with this kind of character much anymore, and when we do they don't get the support they need here. This was once a great school but like the neighborhoods we serve this school has gone downhill" (September 6, 2009).

But sometimes educators work with parents and students to create schools that serve their needs and beat the odds. These are the exceptional schools, places where the culture within is more powerful than the culture and the pull of the streets. Schools that are not only safe and orderly but are places where teaching and learning are respected and revered, and where relationships between students and teachers are premised on a shared commitment to the pursuit of higher goals, and where parents and teachers recognize and act upon their mutual interests. Such schools exist right now (Chenowith, 2009) and their existence is proof, both that it can be done and that the problem facing so many other schools is not the kids.

This volume is about the efforts of educators who have created such schools and about their work in realizing a vision with others. The new schools described in this volume have been created with the deliberate intention of countering the obstacles that commonly undermine urban public schools. Obstacles that come in the form of local, state, and federal policies that place greater emphasis on ranking students and schools on the basis of test scores than on ensuring that all students have the opportunity to learn; obstacles that are created by the "invisible hand" of market forces—forces that revitalize and gentrify some areas while rendering others and their residents destitute and obsolete (Sassen, 1998). These are schools created for "new times": times when human needs are often less important than corporate needs, and the forces of the marketplace play a greater role in shaping the lives of young people than institutions like the family or the church. In these "new times," the stories of educators who are working against great odds to create schools that serve the needs of the most disadvantaged children and communities serve as a potent reminder of what is possible.

The fact that these educators carry out their work in the face of opposition makes their stories that much more compelling. These are schools that encounter opposition from petty bureaucrats who are more concerned with ensuring compliance to procedures than with ensuring that the learning needs of children are met. Opposition from other educators who don't believe that the poor children of color they serve can learn at higher levels and who object to the idea that they should be held accountable for making it happen. That they are able to overcome this opposition makes their stories a source of inspiration for others. This is especially true for those who understand that the effort to create great schools for poor children of color is inherently political, and in these times, understanding the political dynamics that thwart and promote educational equity is as important as understanding curriculum and instruction.

These are the stories of educators who understand that urban education is necessarily work carried out amid a myriad of contradictions. The educators in this volume understand that because urban public schools are vital to the communities they serve, they must be capable of meeting their *educational and social* needs. These are educators who recognize that although urban public schools are often deeply flawed and dysfunctional, they don't have to be, and they are educators who act on the belief that it is possible to create schools that nurture and support the hopes and aspirations of those they serve.

To appreciate a volume like this, one must understand the challenges and contradictions inherent within the political moment in which we find ourselves. After electing the first African American president just 3 years ago, a president who promised "change we can believe in," we find ourselves sobered by the reality that change is slow, sometimes painfully slow, that divided government can produce policy paralysis, and that a prolonged recession can squelch the hopes and dreams of millions. The wars in Iraq and Afghanistan have not ended, health care is still not free or universal, well-paying jobs are scarce, incarceration rates are still high, and the hope we voted for remains elusive. Perhaps our expectations were unrealistic. With our expectations now leveled both by the grim realities of the economy and the administration's politics of pragmatism, instead of inching the dial of social progress forward, we find ourselves resisting efforts to push it backward even further.

This backward march is in some ways most evident in the current policy debates over the future of American education. Prior to his election, President Obama carved out what many regarded as a more progressive and enlightened position on education reform. Recognizing that No Child Left Behind (NCLB) had become widely unpopular due to its overemphasis on standardized tests, he declared ". . . don't tell us that the only way to teach a child is to spend much of the year preparing him to fill in a few bubbles on a standardized test." He pledged to lead the nation in a different direction.

We are still waiting for a change of course. Since the election, the president and his secretary of education, Arne Duncan, have adopted policies that have had far more in common with the previous administration than expected. Market-based reforms like performance pay for teachers, the excessive emphasis on charter schools as alternatives to traditional public schools, and the distribution of federal funds that were once treated as entitlements to compensate for poverty through competitive grants, all represent a disturbing continuity with the policies of the past. The administration does not understand why NCLB failed to do more to improve schools in high poverty communities and consequently it has continued to embrace the failed policies of the past.

While confusion and ideologically driven, fad-oriented policies characterize federal education policy, highly polarized debates over the direction of school reform at the local level permeate debates over educational policy in most American cities. In New York and Los Angeles, highly contentious battles are being waged between teacher unions, school districts, and the local media over the release of test scores that will be publicly tied to teachers. Even though there is widespread agreement that an accurate methodology for linking student test scores to teachers is not available, policymakers and their allies in certain foundations have decided to push ahead with this idea. In Chicago, Washington D.C., and Los Angeles fierce battles are fought between those who see charter schools as a Trojan horse that will lead to the dismantling of public schools, and those who see them as its saviors. In communities like Harlem and cities like Albany in New York, 40% of school-age children are now enrolled in charter schools. In state capitols, politicians wage bitter fights over academic standards, mayoral control of city schools, and most important, budget allocations to cash-strapped school districts.

The debates and conflicts between these warring factions are, of course, not on a level playing field. With the financial backing of hedge fund managers and the Gates and Broad Foundations, a new orthodoxy over what constitutes real reform has emerged. Led by Joel Klein, the former chancellor of New York City; Michelle Rhee, the former chancellor of Washington, D.C.; and Joe Williams of Democrats for Education Reform, this new crop of reformers has argued that "bad teaching" rather than poverty is the primary cause of failure in urban schools. They argue that in order to improve urban public schools, power must be taken away from unions and others who defend the "status quo." Claiming to oppose treating poverty as an excuse for low achievement, Klein and his allies in the Education Equity Project (EEP) wrote the following in the April 9, 2010 edition of the *Washington Post*:

> In the debate over how to fix American public education, many believe that schools alone cannot overcome the impact that economic disadvantage has on a child, that life outcomes are fixed by poverty and family circumstances, and that education doesn't work until other problems are solved. This theory is, in some ways, comforting for educators. . . . Problem is, the theory is wrong. It's hard to know but plenty of evidence demonstrates that schools can make an enormous difference despite the challenges presented by poverty and family background. (p. A19)

Such assertions must be seen as more than merely a matter of political difference. In claiming that poverty is not an issue that must be addressed, educational leaders like Klein and Rhee have chosen to attack teacher unions and ignore the suffering and desperation in America's poorest neighborhoods. They are also ignoring years of research in the social sciences on the effects of poverty, and because they do so, they are unable to understand why the educational reforms implemented over the last 30 years have not succeeded in bringing about sustainable improvements in the most disadvantaged schools. Recent evidence from international comparisons of achievement in math and science (Cavanagh and Manzo, 2009), child health and well-being (UNICEF, 2007), and analyses of the lack of progress made in closing the so-called achievement gap (Barton and Coley, 2010) suggests that greater progress has not been achieved because we have ceased to make a concerted effort to alleviate poverty in American society. Other observers have pointed out that inequity in the types of investments that have the greatest impact on student learning (e.g., universal access to high-quality early childhood education, higher professional standards for teachers, and so on) have not been made, and as a result, many nations have surpassed the United States (e.g., South Korea, Singapore, and Australia) in educational performance (Darling-Hammond, 2010).

As a scholar and an activist, I have found myself in the middle of several of the policy debates. I say the middle because on many of the issues facing urban public schools I find it difficult to position myself at one extreme or the other. I support many charter schools because several of the ones I visit are so much better than the public schools. How could I oppose well-run schools like Democracy Prep in Harlem or North Star in Newark, where nearly all of the students graduate and attend college at levels that put comparable public schools to shame? Only a cynical ideologue could oppose a school like KIPP Aspire Intermediate School in San Antonio, which serves the most disadvantaged children in the barrio, or Community Roots, a progressive charter School in Fort Greene, Brooklyn, one of the few integrated schools in New York City. From the standpoint of policy, I am aware of the threat that charter schools pose to traditional public schools; in many cases, they drain resources and better-prepared students away from public schools. However, I would rather fight to ensure that charter schools are accountable and accessible than shut them down. I know that in many cases they are no better than the public schools and in some cases even worse, but there is a glaring need for new approaches to educating poor children and the best charters are creating models of success from which we should learn. I work with teacher unions to fight against school closures in New York and draconian budget cuts, but I also push them to do more to expedite the evaluation process so that it is less difficult to remove ineffective and incompetent teachers from classrooms. Throughout the country, I work with educators who are searching for ways to improve struggling schools and I always chide them to stop blaming their students or their parents for the school's failings. I refuse to allow the highly polarized politics of school reform to pigeonhole me or box me into a camp. The only camp I want to be part of is the one that is willing to fight like hell for all children to receive a quality education.

To be successful, those who lead the new schools must devise ways to mitigate the harmful effects of poverty on student achievement and child development. They must also challenge the notion that poverty is an insurmountable obstacle to student achievement or a learning disability. They must do this by not allowing the unmet needs of poor children to become an obstacle to learning or an excuse for their own ineffectiveness. They must form partnerships with community organizations that can help them in meeting student needs and they must devise strategies and interventions to counter the ways in which poverty can undermine learning and child development. I strongly disagree with the regimentation that the "No Excuses" advocates have come to believe is essential for educating poor children, but as a teacher who has worked in extremely challenging schools I recognize that some poor children do need to acquire social skills that will make it possible for them to navigate multiple social settings, embrace the importance of hard work, and in many cases some poor children need structured school environments where limits and expectations are clear. Finally, I recognize that accountability is essential, but not the type prescribed by most policymakers, which is based largely on student test scores. Rather, the accountability that research shows has the greatest impact on learning is mutual and reciprocal, and clearly lays out what is expected from all parties—teachers, parents, administrators, and students. Without this, it is almost impossible for schools serving poor children to succeed.

The new schools for these new times cannot be like the schools of the past. They can't operate on the assumption that failure is acceptable for some, and they can't continue to bore children to sleep by stressing basic skills and rote learning. To be the vital community assets that our communities and society so desperately need, the new schools must approach teaching and learning differently. They must prepare their students by cultivating their talents and nurturing their imaginations. They must treat teachers as intellectual workers and provide them with the support they need to be effective. They must respect the parents they serve as genuine partners and collaborators, regardless of how much money they earn, how much education they have, or the language they speak. They must do all of this because there is simply no other way for our schools to be successful in these times. And they must do so because so much is at stake. The schools we have will ultimately play a role in determining what type of society we will live in and what our future will be like. Creating schools that make it possible for us to look to the future with a sense of optimism rather than fear is indeed a tall order and clearly one that not all who venture into this work will be able to carry out, but it is the work that must be done because our future depends on it.

Pedro Noguera

NOTES

1. Bryk, Sebring, et al. (2010); Anyon (1997); Payne (1984).

REFERENCES

Anyon, J. (1997) *Ghetto schooling: A political economy of urban educational reform*. New York: Teachers College Press..

Barton, P. E., & Coley, R. J. (2010). *The black-white achievement gap: When progress stopped*. Princeton, NJ: Education Testing Service.

Bryk, A., Sebring, P. B., et al. (2010). *Organizing schools for improvement: Lessons from Chicago*. Chicago: University of Chicago Press.

Cavanagh, S., & Manzo, K. K. (2009, April 21). International Exams Yield Less-Than-Clear Lessons. *Education Week, 28*(29), 1, 16–17.

Chenowith, K. (2009). *How it's being done: Urgent lessons from unexpected schools*. Cambridge, MA: Harvard Education Press.

Darling-Hammond, L. (2010). *The flat world and education: How America's commitment to equity will determine our future*. New York: Teachers College Press.

Klein, J., Lomax, M., & Muraguia, J. (2010, April 9). Poverty is not the answer. *Washington Post*, p. A19

Sassen, S. (1998). *The mobility of labor and capital: A study in international investment and labor flow*. Cambridge, UK: Cambridge University Press.

Stone, C. N., et al. (2001). *Building civic capacity: The politics of reforming urban schools*. Lawrence: University of Kansas Press.

UNICEF. (2007). Child poverty in perspective: An overview of child well-being in rich countries. *Innocenti Report Card, 7*.

Payne, C. (1984). *The ambiguity of success and failure in urban education*. Santa Barbara: Greenwood Publishing Group.

Wilson, W. J. (1987). *The truly disadvantaged: The inner city, the underclass and public policy*. Chicago: University of Chicago Press

Part I

1974–1998

It wasn't exactly China's Let a Thousand Flowers Bloom, but beginning in the mid-1970s there was a proliferation of new small schools at a rate and of a variety unprecedented in the history of American education. At the heart of what was to become a movement was Deborah Meier's Central Park East Elementary School, later to be joined by its high school sibling, Central Park East Secondary School. CPE offered an alternative to the way children were taught and the way their learning was assessed that brought visitors from all over the country to see with their own eyes that progressive education was not the exclusive domain of wealthy private and suburban schools. Urban Academy offered another stunning alternative to secondary education constructed around inquiry and argumentation.

What these schools and those which sought to emulate them had in common was a deep commitment to social justice, to overcoming the inequities in the educational system that kept poor children of color out of the winner's circle forever. CPE and Urban Academy were born before charter schools were a proverbial twinkle in the eye of reformers of all political stripes. As Ann Cook says in her piece about the birth of Urban Academy, with all the recent talk about the entrepreneurial spirit in the charter school movement, the true entrepreneurs were the teachers, practitioners, and others close to the ground who created schools that seized on opportunities to do things that hadn't been done before for populations that had not been served well by existing schools—poor children of color (CPE, NKO), dropouts and potential dropouts (MET and Urban Academy), formerly incarcerated youth (Maya Angelou). Unlike so many of the later new school founders, they had no desire to undermine the existing public school system. In fact, in the case of

1

the North Kenwood Oakland Charter School, its original mission was to serve as a professional development site for struggling public schools, an effort to strengthen public education, rather than destroy it. Nor were they seeking to break the teacher unions, a goal, implicit or explicit, of most of the new charter school operators. In fact, most of the schools in this section, though not all, are union schools, committed to supporting teachers' rights to organize.

It's important to note that most of the schools in the second section of the book were inspired by those that went before them and built on their accomplishments. What distinguishes them from their predecessors is the star under which they were born, an environment more data driven, more open to the standardization efforts of large charter management organizations than to the visions of practicing teachers, more results and data driven (or as a friend said, data driven to distraction). So, hail to the pioneers and hail to those who came after them and managed to prevail against a rising tide of corporatized education.

Central Park East School

Starting Out with Small Schools

DEBORAH MEIER

Full disclosure: I have very limited experience in anything but a small school—starting at age 4. And I have never been the founder or principal of a big school that I turned into a small one or ones. So I speak out of a certain level of ignorance, which can be useful, but be forewarned.

On September 8, 1989, the *New York Times* put the following bold statement by me on their Op-Ed page:

> I love New York, I love Chicago. I love Beethoven's "Ninth Symphony." It's not an antipathy to bigness that makes me a fervent champion of small schools. Rather it's the conviction that unless we start thinking small, none of the recent consensus that has developed around needed reforms is remotely feasible. Small schools are not the answer, but without them none of the proposed answers stand a chance.

I think it may have been the first such public statement for a lay audience on the subject of small schools. Given the response I received, I realized later that I had articulated what was on the minds of many of the existing small schools people—who were often, if anything, embarrassed at being small. We were generally dismissed by our colleagues and policy folks alike as being a "cute" but irrelevant sideshow to *real reform*.

Nearly 20 years later, small schools are the reform of the day, and a day doesn't pass that I don't hear of another district starting new small schools, mostly high schools, generally out of large existing ones. And now it's I who've turned skeptic!

Starting Up, edited by Lisa Arrastia and Marvin Hoffman. Copyright © 2012 by Teachers College, Columbia University. All rights reserved. Prior to photocopying items for classroom use, please contact the Copyright Clearance Center, Customer Service, 222 Rosewood Dr., Danvers, MA 01923, USA, tel. (978) 750-8400, www.copyright.com.

I got a call from a 600-pupil high school in a middle-class community recently, asking me if I'd come and talk about the school breaking down into smaller academies. I said no. But I told them that I'd be happy to come in to talk about good schooling and the ways in which they think they are still missing the mark. We'll do, it seems, almost anything to avoid talking about what it is we cherish, care about, believe in, and thus, what schools are intended to "pass on" to the future citizens of the community, that is, the community writ small as well as large, even large enough to consider the whole planet. When the school pressed me, I told them that my experience suggests that breaking up a big school into small ones would require several years of organizational work, involving many complex discussions about how to divide the staff, what to call the schools, how to reorganize the building, degrees of autonomy and forms of governance, and just the little things like who gets which rooms and whose friendship circles are destroyed, and on and on. All of these are critical, but . . . they don't get to the heart of the matter: what's going on between kids, between kids and adults, and between adults, and how these add up to education!

Every school I was involved in starting was located within a big building, and shared space with other schools serving many different age groups. Looking back nostalgically at what it takes to start a school, there are some obvious essentials: Ideas, colleagues, and enormous energy—those are the ABCs; it probably helps to know one's terrain—the political and communal traditions, the people who carry weight, the rules that may get in the way (but not too much of that or you'll get discouraged before you start).

I began Central Park East (CPE), the first of a series of small K–6 elementary schools in East Harlem, because Tony Alvarado, the superintendent of District 2, asked if I'd like to. That enabled me to shortcut a lot of the politics I've laid down above. Because Alvarado was the superintendent in East Harlem at a time when district superintendents had a lot of autonomy and power; what he wanted, he got. So he got me, and four of my friends, who in the fall of 1974 had an idea sufficient, at least, for urban public education, and a staff that consisted of highly experienced teachers. It seemed a good bet to Alvarado as a place to launch his ambitious agenda.

We spent the late spring and fall planning, scrounging for supplies (we didn't know about budgets and ordering), talking to Head Start and nursery schools in the area, and putting up signs in local housing projects. We were a group of friends who had met through City College's Workshop Center for Open Education and had hit it off. We all had experience, we thought alike—or sort of—and we were racially diverse. We included one African American, one Latino, and two whites. The students who trickled into our cozy space in the corner of a fairly large neighborhood elementary school on 103rd Street included, to our surprise, a few middle-class whites, but mostly Latino and African American children, many of whom were indirectly "sent" to us by professionals who thought we might be the right place for these hyperactive, difficult, demanding families and students. We took in kindergarten, first- and second-graders, plus a few third-graders (who had siblings in the lower grades) with a plan to go up a grade per year. Our classes were inter-age—two kindergarten/first-grade classes and one second- and third-grade class. And, no office, just an answering machine.

The first challenge was proving that our kind of progressive schooling had an audience among low-income African American and Latino families in East Harlem. The viewpoint that we shared wasn't entirely spelled out, even among ourselves. What we shared was a belief that what was good for the elite was also good for the least advantaged. We wanted all kids to have an education fit for a ruling class, which in a democracy should be everyone. We wanted to offer unconditional respect to teachers, students, and their families. We wanted to create an authentic interpersonal community of learners of all ages who, together, explored the wonders of the world within a safe setting of competent adults.

Perhaps it was my own personal history with progressive schooling, and my dismay at the kind of public schooling I saw my own children get in New York City, as well as what I saw in the central Harlem school in which I first taught that impelled me. It gave me confidence that spilled over onto those we came in contact with. In addition, I had spent 5 years at P.S. 144 in New York City creating a small four-room wing (pre-kindergarten–second grade) modeled on what we then called "open education." During those 4 years I spent at the Workshop Center at City College led by Lillian Weber, I met many other people who shared my beliefs.

Aside from providing support and conviction, the Workshop Center also provided me with colleagues to start the venture. Every one of us was an experienced teacher—the least experienced had 3 years under her belt, the most experienced nearly 20. We all came from the same "center" of thought and were sure we agreed on almost everything. Of course, we didn't, but our language was close enough to provide a common front to interested families.

It took a while for us to become interesting to families that had experienced success in school, or who anticipated that their youngsters were school-ready. Head Start centers and our neighboring public schools urged parents whose kids seemed "difficult" to try us.

We were welcoming. But it was slow going. We didn't reach our promised goal of 100 students until well into the year, and Alvarado never pressed us on it or threatened to remove staff. Fortunately, in the first 2 years we shared three floors of a building wing with another principal who was an ally and co-thinker. After this principal left and was replaced by an ambitious and very traditional one, we realized how lucky we had been not to have to deal with the problem of an uncooperative principal in the beginning as we struggled with opening dilemmas.

Despite our openness, some parents were startled by the school: all the animals (including a smelly ferret), the absence of 30 desks with a teacher desk in front, and all the art materials, plus all the beautiful but unregulated books. There were books everywhere—books about architecture and cities in the block area, books about plants and animals in the science area, storybooks in the rug area, and lots of beautiful materials for drawing and painting and representing the world around us. And we were out of the building as often as we found an excuse to do so—being next to Central Park, a skating rink, trails in the woods and rocks for climbing, and easy walking distance from several world famous and amazing museums.

But there were also contentious issues about "discipline," about the role of parents, about when we needed to be on the same page, and so on, and we weren't sure how to solve them. We were all in the classroom—with a recording machine in our "office" that announced that all the adults were busy with kids, leave a number and we'll call back later. We met every day before and after classes and argued over discipline and curriculum and who made what decisions. I was the presumed "leader"—chosen by the district—but we operated collectively. During our second year, in the midst of a difficult start-up month, because the city was laying off staff (thousands of teachers lost their jobs), and some of ours were hanging on by a thin thread, we lost our solidarity when confronted with a group of dissatisfied parents. They wanted more of a voice in what and how we ran the school, more African American studies, and some wanted less of the first-name stuff and less openness to questions about sex. We didn't all give the same answers when we met with these parents, and no one was paying full-time attention to the issues being raised.

Again, an unfriendly administration could have nailed us at the start. It would have been easy to make use of the divisions within the staff, and the lack of confidence in my leadership expressed by some parents (not entirely unwarranted since I was hardly being a leader) could easily have ended our glorious experiment in Year 2. Instead, the district came to our rescue. They said they had full confidence in me and in the premises of the school, and offered to find alternatives within the district that were more to their liking for any dissatisfied staff and parents, as small schools of choice were beginning to blossom throughout the district. Two teachers and about a dozen parents left. I agreed to leave the classroom and take on larger oversight of the school rather than the narrower tunnel vision of my classroom.

That was the big crisis moment. It was also the moment we added two very experienced teachers, including a topnotch old hand at this approach to schooling for our fifth and sixth grade. This was critical because anxiety about moving on to junior high was surely part of parental distress.

Central Park East became so popular that two replicas started in 1978 and 1983: Central Park East II and River East. I was principal of CPE I and II for the first 2 years, which was both wise and unwise. It made it easier to be sure that neither school was conceived of as the "real" CPE. The three, over time, of course, developed their own personas, although we tried (unsuccessfully) to be so much alike that we could accept kids centrally and place them in any one of the three. We even had some transferring of teachers. We met regularly and worked hard to avoid being treated differently by the district office, so that we kept no secrets from each other and discussed differences before we committed ourselves to them. Over time, this too was watered down, as new directors came and went at CPE II and River East and the schools more and more had their own agenda with the district. Maybe *this* was inevitable since we were purposely intended to be small and democratic.

In 1985, we started a 7–12 grade school for the graduates of CPE I, II, and River East. It was a very different experience for a host of reasons. Above all, none of us had any good models of what progressive education might look like for our students at these ages. The best New York City private elementary schools often didn't look very "open" in high school; they often shed their least successful students as "unfit" for their school's mission. We had no intention of doing either, and this is dramatically different for most new schools today. We hired only very experienced staff—most with more than 10 years in New York City public schools. Although they all saw themselves as somewhat innovative teachers, virtually none had experience with progressive schooling. But designing a Coalition of Essential Schools education, with multi-age classes, 2 hour-long blocks, and close contact with families, with the promise that they would have to "demonstrate" their readiness to graduate at ages 17–19, presented real challenges. None of us knew what we were doing. But once again, we had a powerful ally in the high school alternative school superintendency, which had been created by the New York City Board of Education, and was led by a remarkable man, Steve Phillips, who was alternately well liked by the central office and also in conflict with them. But Phillips stood firm. In addition, the reputation of Ted Sizer, the founder of the Coalition of Essential Schools, helped pave the way for our acceptance, and he came to town each time a new superintendent arrived. I also got a MacArthur award as a "genius" at the end of the 2nd year of CPE Secondary School (CPESS). This was the first

MacArthur Genius award to go to a school educator. It was perfectly timed, and although I got no congratulatory message from the Central Headquarters, I did win my first critical battle, probably in part because of the publicity surrounding the award.

Over the next decade, I helped many others start similar secondary or high schools. It seemed to be a genie that could never be rebottled. Some were more experimental in name than in substance, but all shared a closer-knit feeling of community. Our euphoria lasted a decade. By the 1990s, the drive toward "standardization" was picking up steam, and the alternative school network was weakened in the process. No other new schools were provided the start-up support (including money) that CPESS had for the first years. Many were required to take in the full age-range of students while we had started one grade at a time. Many of these new schools did not have the same ability to draw on experienced teachers, while some preferred young teachers in the belief that old-timers would be harder to teach new tricks. By the late 1990s none of the start-up high schools had the freedom over curriculum and graduation requirements that we did. And many started in terrible, overcrowded sites, or were forced to move several times in their opening years. Many survived, some didn't. And almost all were forced to make dispiriting compromises that left people feeling less powerful and adventurous. What's amazing is that most are still striving out there, with some of their original leaders in place, and they are refusing to give in.

When I left NYC in 1996 for the Annenberg Institute in Rhode Island, I had time to think and speak and write. But within a year, I was missing the schoolhouse. As I drove to Boston for an interview about my new book, *The Power of Their Ideas: Lessons for America from a Small School in Harlem* (Beacon Press, 2002), I had an idea. Why not start a K–8 school and re-explore elementary education in a new setting among so many of my Cambridge and Boston friends? The idea came at a perfect moment. The big ambitious plan we had for New York City—a "pilot" learning zone of 50,000 students and 150 schools had been shot down. But Boston was launching a smaller version—a network of pilot schools that would be part of the Boston public school system yet would operate under charter-like conditions. It was a chance to be part of some exciting adventure while I could focus not on the politics of it, but the nitty-gritty of starting a new school.

*   *   *   *   *   *

Every city has its own history, and every cluster of adults brings with them their own stories. Mission Hill in Boston began with grades K–3: four classrooms and five teachers. Simplicity itself. But while the teachers were all experienced, few had experience with low-income and African American or Latino kids. The only progressive education that existed was in suburban and Cambridge schools or a small string of private independent schools. But once again, as with CPE, we started with a staff that included three "minority" teachers—two African American and one Latina teacher. The school attracted some whites from nearby Jamaica Plain, but from the start students were accepted by lottery through a complex integration plan that was part of the Boston public system itself. Officially, we had more flexibility and freedom from rules than ever before. Usually, we had just acted without constraints, hoping the results would warn off critics. But this time the pilot agreement between Boston's management and union offered that freedom and flexibility to us up front, which made our work easier and less cumbersome. It meant that as principal I didn't need to worry about what to share and what not to, how to cover my tracks, and other deceptions that I was accustomed to.

But the old "parent problems" re-emerged in a particular Boston fashion. Among the middle-class families who came to Mission Hill (which was the name we chose based on our location in the former Catholic school of the same name) were many former leaders of earlier struggles for integration, equity, and freedom from unfriendly fire from Boston's bureaucracy. They were experts at protecting parental and student rights, and inclined toward suspicions. While our "constitution"—unlike in New York City, we were obliged to have one that we created—gave parents, staff, and community each a third of the membership on the board, and this body was responsible ultimately for the school's funds, organization, and evaluation (including hiring and firing the principal), each constituency was nervous about its rights. Parents above all. The staff had enormous formal and informal daily power; the power of parents was more secondhand. The issues between them were rarely substantive, but still intensely felt. Probably most parents were largely unaware of these issues; they were mostly worrying about whether the school was properly preparing their own individual child. But this tension complicated our growing years. Meanwhile, while the school always had a substantial number of teachers of color (far more than most Boston schools), the black/white issue remained just below the surface of many disputes, and our attempts to surface them rarely were as successful as we imagined they ought to be.

The advent of the No Child Left Behind age put new pressure on the school, as most schools focused more and more on test-prep and Mission Hill refused to bend. The parents and staff were united on this, but unlike the pre-NCLB days, the power no longer rested with our own constituents. Low test scores now meant threatened action from the state, and loyalty to the school now seemed to require "doing something" about test scores. In subtle ways, this changed the nature of the staff's professional discussions. There were 4 to 5 hours a week of staff meeting and this NCLB ethos made serious inroads into how that time was spent.

As with the CPE schools in New York City, despite the pilot status, keeping the school secure still meant spending time making powerful friends and allies. We needed people "downtown" who interpreted rules and regulations—which didn't disappear with pilot status—in friendly ways, or who alerted us to potential conflicts. "Downtown" meant both management and labor. It also meant building an organization, the Center for Collaborative Education (CCE), to fight many of our fights for us as pilots. But in turn we needed to spend some time nurturing and supporting CCE, though the level of help we needed was less and mostly different. We no longer required as many hours squeezing ourselves into odd shapes so that we could pretend we were staying in line.

I think there are several critical lessons to be learned in starting a new small school. Despite our uniqueness in some ways, it's clear to me that successful new small schools need to start with a core of like-minded and self-confident, experienced practitioners, even just three to four. They need to avoid bending every time a crisis arises or compromising their ideas in order to "get along." The pull of gravity is strong and the solution to a crisis is more often moving farther and faster toward one's vision, rather than retreating from it.

They also need to work out ways to have plenty of time for faculty to be together, and they need to ensure there is a faculty small enough to hear each other speak over and over around a common table. Some way has to be found to get at least the teaching staff to spend many hours together without the kids (e.g., at retreats), but also every week. There is no way to avoid the time crunch. Even little problems turn into big ones if solving them is postponed.

They need to take the time, early on, to get to know each other's classrooms and styles of teaching. It may make them uneasy at first, but getting in that habit is hard to put into place "later."

The time spent on working out relationships with the families of one's own students—and there being such a thing as "one's own"—has to be built into the school. Through all the turmoil between the official school and official parent body, the backbone is those other relationships that remain sturdy and strong.

And finally, whatever schedule, statement of objectives, curriculum, or organization—it pays to make it very simple. The simpler, the better, so that the people involved can spend their attention on getting right what cannot be simplified. All the individuals we need to work together with, and the complex ideas we are trying to learn ourselves and teach to kids, that's where the time has to be focused. Decision making needs to be simple and easy, not cumbersome and requiring lots of committees and subcommittees and referrals to external bodies. Space needs to be clear and simple—who belongs where and when. The more the space can be shared so that it's easy to observe each other's business, the better. And the "who's responsible" for what needs to be simple. In the end, what counts most is that the vast majority of the adults in the building take it for granted that "they" are responsible. Open, publicly accessible criticism kept CPE as well as Mission Hill, and any good public institution, always prepared to be a learning institution not just for students, but for the entire school community; that was key. It's a tension that can be unnerving, exactly as it must be in the larger institutions of democracy. One never has it exactly right, which means that it must everlastingly rebalance, over and over again.

I watch, visit, and read about lots of new small schools and I'm amazed at how many of these points are ignored by those who do the "planning." I still suspect that over the long, long haul most of them are better for most kids than the schools they replaced (although probably not all). But it still amazes me how little current school policy either rests on the experiences of those who pioneered this work or on the wisdom of other experienced educators. Most of the current "reformers" once again reject our original proposition that the kind of mutual and unconditional respect that schools for the wealthy take for granted won't serve "other people's children" well. It's as though they said, "Now that we agree on small schools, it's business and finance and organizational expertise that is needed to bring it to scale. Your way, they often patronizingly reminded me, was slow and careful, but we haven't the time or resources for that. If we left it to those 'who know best,' we'd miss this window in time. Full steam ahead; and teachers or parents who don't jump on will just be jumped over or on."

Perhaps. We shall have to wait and see.

2

North Kenwood Oakland Charter School

*Small Gestures and Sturdy Nests—
The Making of NKO*

MARVIN HOFFMAN

You know the old movie—was it Mickey Rooney and Judy Garland?—where they say "Hey, let's find a barn and do a show." That's the way a lot of people approach wanting to start a new school. I doubt that I was ever quite that naïve, but I don't think I had any clear idea about what it was going to take to get a new school off the ground when I started down the path that led to the creation of the North Kenwood Oakland Charter School. In the best of all possible worlds, a new school should emerge full-born from the hearts of caring teachers and parents with visions of a better way for teachers to teach and children to learn, but there's a lot of reality that gets in the way.

For several years, I've been a judge in a kind of fair at a nearby suburban high school that is the culmination of a course in which students are asked, in teams, to design the charter school of their dreams. They are students in a pretty good school, so their designs often remain surprisingly close to the educations that got them here. However, I find myself, by turns, charmed and irritated by the flights of fancy that they do generate—schools where all subjects are taught through the arts, where class sizes don't exceed ten, or where each homeroom has its own college counselor. The irritation stems from the fact that their teacher has freed them from the responsibility of generating a budget to support their grand ideas. I understand that he chooses to allow their visions to take flight unfettered by the burdens of dollars or government regulations or high-stakes testing. I like to think that I have emerged from the process of starting and operating a school unjaded, still able to become intoxicated by a strong new vision of schooling, but confronting the work of these young idealists, I am quick to ask, "Where are they going to find the money to pay all those counselors? What are they prepared to give up instead?" or "What colleges are their students going to be able to get into without grades?" It's those nagging questions that make me wonder what collateral damage I've suffered in the course of doing the thing itself. Or is it better seen not as damage, but as accumulated wisdom?

As I'm writing this piece, I'm engaged in a parallel process intended to inform the writing. I am listening to an audio diary that I kept during the year and a half from the time we began preparing an application for a charter from the Chicago Public Schools through the first year of the school's operation. Every night when I sat down to dinner with my wife, I turned on the tape recorder and unburdened myself of the events of the day. (When I revealed the existence of the diary to a colleague, he said, "I'm less impressed by the existence of the diary than I am by the fact that you sat down to dinner with your wife every night.") There are 50 hours of these tapes, and when I become impatient with the listening, I adjourn to my computer and begin to write.

Now into the seventh 90-minute tape, I'm still nowhere near the opening of the school. If I were to be the kind of social scientist who codes diary material systematically, the most sparsely populated cells would be those labeled "Instruction" or "Children" or "Learning." The tally marks would inhabit boxes the existence of which I had not been aware a few short months earlier: "Real Estate," Fire Codes," "Sprinkler Systems," things you could argue are necessary preconditions to learning, but are so burdensome in the attention they require that they drain the energy needed to maintain focus on the main purpose of the enterprise.

I was luckier than most in the support I had. Our school, the North Kenwood Oakland Charter School (NKO), grew out of work that had been ongoing at the University of Chicago for a decade. A word about the school's name. It was a placeholder in our written proposals. Our intention was to choose a more compelling name once kids and parents were in place, so that they could have a voice in the selection, but once the first T-shirts and sweatpants were ordered with NKO emblazoned on them, the name was fixed like a photo image emerging from its chemical bath. Representing the school by the community it served didn't turn out to be a bad idea, though we remained jealous of schools that had grabbed more dramatic names—Polaris, Galapagos, Catalyst.

The Center for School Improvement had been engaged through that decade with helping networks of Chicago Public Schools improve their reading and writing instruction. The situation was nothing less than desperate. It was a time when all a school had to do to stay off probation was to have more than 20% of its students reading at grade level. The Center's efforts were not as effective as they could have been because it was not in control of the many factors, often dictated from downtown, which served to undermine the practices highlighted in the professional development the Center was offering (the required textbooks, the mandated assessments, and so on). We came to believe that the only way to proceed with our work was to have our own school where the practices we were advocating, what has come to be known over the years as "balanced literacy" could be implemented in purer form without the usual undermining forces at work.

The time is 1997. The charter law had just been passed by the Illinois state legislature the year before, over substantial opposition from the unions, which had serious problems with their limited capacity to organize teachers in charter schools. Because of the pressure they brought to bear, the number of charters for Chicago was capped at 15.

The union opposition to charters was a cause of some anguish and soul searching for me and for others involved in proposing the new school. In spite of growing disillusionment with the teacher unions—many of whose practices and policies seemed to place the interests and needs of teachers ahead of those of children, parents, and communities—a number of us at the Center came from strong union families, or families favorably disposed to unions. We maintained our sentimental attachments to the institution. This made it difficult for us to align ourselves with a concept that was so clearly anathema to unions and the political leaders who supported them. But charter schools appeared to be the only route for attaining the freedom over curriculum, hiring, scheduling, and the allocation of resources we needed to create the kind of school we were seeking.

One of the reasons unions and their liberal and radical allies so strongly opposed charters was the belief that they were the Trojan horses for vouchers and privatization efforts aimed at dismantling the public school system. They had good reason to be fearful. From the beginning, charter school advocates have been a motley collection of strange bedfellows, many of whom were after exactly what charter opponents suspected. That didn't happen to be true in our case. Growing out of the Center's previous work supporting struggling Chicago Public Schools, we aspired to be a resource for strengthening existing public schools, not undermining them. It was that commitment that, for me at least, made the choice of a "non-union" course defensible.

In any case, competition for charters was fierce because the school system, following a phased plan, was only intending to open five new schools in that second year, on the heels of the initial five approved the previous year, but there were 19 applicants. The Center's intended leap from being a program that served existing schools to being the operator of one's own school was formidable, and like most proposals, ours contained a strong element of fiction, right down to the attached petitions signed by parents who might potentially be interested in enrolling their children. These names were gathered in haste, often from people who barely had any idea what our school plan was about.

As late as several weeks before the submission deadline, we were not certain that we were going to move forward with the proposal at all. We were wrestling with what is arguably the single most bedeviling problem for aspiring new schools—facilities. Several of the schools approved in the first year failed to find a suitable site and never opened. At the 11th hour, we found a church building in our target community that, with a bit of imagination and a bunch of money could become a school. The church, a dying congregation in a once grand community, had an attached education building, complete with gym, which had served its membership in better days. My earlier remarks about becoming an expert in real estate, fire codes, and sprinkler systems are all wrapped up in that dinosaur of a building. Once we had passed through the rather stringent review process that had been created to screen charter school applicants, that building consumed my energies and the attention of half a dozen people from the Center and the university for a number of months.

Unlike Mickey and Judy and their show in a barn, it becomes more and more difficult to start a new school without some kind of benefactor, a sugar daddy who can foot some of the initial bills and provide the expertise—instructional and otherwise—to get you through the bumpy start-up. In this case, the sugar daddy was the university and as the projected costs of getting the building up to standards rose into the stratosphere of half a million dollars, a figure that would turn out to be close to our entire first year's budget, the university reluctantly took up those costs, on the understanding that much of the money would be repaid and the school would not become dependent long term on the largesse of the university. As the folks at Harvard like to say about their associated schools, "Every tub on its own bottom."

Every action, individual or institutional, is driven by a complex web of motivations. The university's support of NKO, which 14 years later has grown into the operation of a mini school system of four charter schools, is no exception. Like many urban universities, the University of Chicago has a history of contentious relationships with its surrounding communities. Expansion needs, the desire to maintain local property values, and the need to ensure a safe physical environment for students and staff led the university to carry out a radical urban renewal program in the 1950s, which was preceded by its participation in restrictive covenant arrangements to keep blacks out of the Hyde Park community throughout the 1940s and threatened encroachment into the neighboring Woodlawn community in the 1960s. There was a considerable reservoir of anger toward the university among its black neighbors, and there's no doubt that the support of a university-sponsored school serving children of color from those communities was an attempt to dispel some of that animosity. But, as a former president of the university said to his trustees, it was also "the right thing to do." Whatever the motivation, it provided those of us who had conceived of the school an opening that suited our needs perfectly.

One of my most vivid memories of the start-up work involved the elaborate process we designed for interviewing every single family that applied for the inaugural grades, even though the lottery process was going to disqualify some of them and prevent them from joining our tiny school community. Nonetheless, we sat with each applicant family, the child plus single parent, mother and father, grandparents, foster parents, aunties—whoever presented themselves—and posed questions about the child's previous school experiences, talents, allergies. For new schools, it's the angel that's in the details. Every gesture of caring, every plate of cookies proffered, every warm greeting at the door, signals to parents and children what kind of institution they are buying into. There is no doubt in my mind that those one-on-one encounters set the tone of our school for years to come and won the loyalty of the families who had basked in that rare moment of institutional warmth and caring.

A strong teaching staff is the make-or-break determinant of the success and viability of a new school. That will come as no surprise to any reader. The questions are where to find them and what are the attributes that define their strength. We were in the fortunate position of piggybacking on the work of the Center for School Improvement, which, in the course of its work with the eight or nine schools in its network, had trained a sizable corps of teachers in the use of what we called then the literacy framework, probably more familiar to current readers as the workshop approach or balanced literacy. We knew the teachers in those schools whose practice was strong, but could we be justified in pirating them from those needy schools where talented replacements would be hard to come by? Andy Hargreaves (Hargreaves & Fink, 1995) believes that new institutions need to operate on the principle of "Do no harm," meaning that they should not weaken existing institutions in the course of creating themselves. We probably rate a B on that criterion. Two of our original four teachers came from those network schools, but we made the case with their principals that they were teachers looking to make a move in any case, and by our hiring them, we could keep them in the network and enable them to be an eventual professional development resource for their home schools.

Perhaps our most important decision about hiring and staff was to seek experienced teachers, whose years in the classroom would enable them to ride through the rough spots that even the best-planned start-up was sure to encounter. Most new schools lean in the opposite direction, recruiting young, often inexperienced teachers in the belief that their energy and enthusiasm would be an asset in enduring the long days and the multiplicity of roles a new school calls for. There is also a budgetary imperative that drives the decision to pursue young teachers who command lower salaries and impose less strain on the meager budgets of charter schools. In Chicago, that budget of $5,300 per child, in contrast to suburban figures double and triple that amount, multiplied by our starting population of 110 students—more about them in a minute—didn't buy a lot of caviar, so, given the fact that we had made a commitment up front to pay our teachers the same starting salaries that the union had negotiated for its membership, the temptation to skimp on the salary line by recruiting novices was great.

The racial composition of that initial teacher team was very much in the forefront of our thinking. We weren't going to hire any teacher *just* because she was black, but we had to cast our nets wide to find the best teachers of both races. Given the fact that the school was sponsored by what everyone identified as a white academic institution and that its initial administrative leadership was white, a significant presence of black teachers was critical for achieving credibility with parents and community. Many black parents would nod their heads in agreement with this surprising statement from Dr. Martin Luther King:

> I favor integration on buses and in all areas of public accommodation and travel. . . . However, I think integration in our public schools is different. In that setting you are dealing with one of the most important assets of an individual—the mind. white people view Black people as inferior. . . . People with such a low view of the Black race cannot be given free rein and put in charge of the intellectual care and development of our boys and girls. (Freedman, 2004, p. 28)

The decision to opt for experience proved to be one of our best. As predicted, the veteran teachers provided the stability and teacherly wisdom we so desperately needed in those early years and won the confidence of many wary parents who weren't sure just what they had signed on for. All the teachers, both black and white—there were two of each—were experienced in working with the almost entirely African American population the school served. The young white teachers who staff most start-ups are simultaneously learning the craft and learning how to navigate in new cultural waters, a formidable duo of challenges. Two of those original four teachers are still at the school after 14 years, belying the reputation charters have of high staff turnover; that speaks volumes about the wisdom of that early decision.

Part of what those veteran teachers were buying into was the promise of a professional community different from the stagnant top-down cultures of the public schools in which they had been serving. Teachers were to have a significant voice in decision making. They would be treated as professionals who were entitled to a full 50-minute lunch break, while other staff members attended to their students in the cafeteria and the playground, in contrast to the hurried 20-minute lunch periods imposed on their public school colleagues. They would be provided with opportunities to participate in the kind of professional development that would deepen their practice. And they would have access to a career ladder that promised additional income and increased and varied responsibilities without extracting them entirely from the classroom environments they loved.

Another crucial part of being treated as professionals involved not just income, but the kind of benefits employees were offered, both teaching and non-teaching staff, both professionals and paraprofessionals. At an early board meeting that first year, the administrative team proposed that, in spite of our meager budget, our health-care coverage should extend to part-time employees as well as our full-time staff. Whatever the financial hit, we argued, it would send a powerful message about what kind of community we intended to be, what kinds of ethical and moral principles we intended to stand behind. Mr. Hudson, our maintenance head, was the first beneficiary of that commitment. Soon after the board endorsed our proposal, he fell ill and was able to receive full coverage for an illness that would otherwise have bankrupted him. Our action on health care had created in him a life-long commitment to the school in gratitude for an act of institutional caring. For teachers and staff, their benefits were similar to those received by University of Chicago employees, and with that reassurance teachers were freed to focus on the main business of the day—teaching.

The downside of the experience that teachers brought from their years in the system was an acculturation to that very top-down system from which they were separating. They were not accustomed to being called upon to participate in budget or scheduling decisions, sometimes preferring to grumble about what my colleagues or I at the Center for School Improvement had decided. Being invited to participate in decision making was often perceived as a sign of weak leadership. Besides, teachers were skeptical about the sincerity of the invitation, just as are students who find themselves with teachers who offer them choices, something they've never experienced before. It takes some convincing that the offer is for real and there are no consequences for acting on it.

Although they overcame much of this reluctance over the years, there were areas where the teachers were absolutely right to resist being drawn into greater decision-making roles. I had created a whole battery of committees and asked that each staff member participate in two of their choice. The leadership of the Center disagreed with my approach to delegating so much responsibility to the teachers, arguing that in the early years of the school, this work needed to be in the hands of the school director, while the teachers focused on the all-important business of getting their instruction in order. Teachers were already extended to the breaking point, working days 2 hours longer than their public school colleagues, and, in the early years, keeping to a 12-month work schedule, with a scant 2 weeks off in the summer.

I should have recognized and remedied sooner the additional burdens I had imposed on the staff, but I was also concerned about the fact that if this pattern of distributive leadership was not in place from the start, it would never take root as part of the school culture, as it has over the years. In this sense, my critics and I were both right to some degree.

I've mentioned in passing that the state's charter laws called for an open lottery process that was intended to give every child in the city an equal shot at admission. The law was intended to prevent charters from engaging in selective admissions practices, such as the cherry-picking of elite students. The irony is that these restrictions prevented us from favoring the poor and working-class students we were most eager to serve. We wanted to demonstrate that, if provided with a rigorous academic program with high expectations, these students of color could be successful academically.

At the same time, the lottery had the hidden benefit of insulating us from pressure from people of influence seeking admission for their kin. Even the alderman's granddaughter had to enter the lottery, where she was not selected. Over the years, we were offered some intriguing lottery-busting offers from eager applicants—more security from the beat cop for our area who was eager for her child to attend, special computer services from a high-tech supplicant, and more. To stick to the principle of an unbiased lottery, particularly in a place like Chicago, with its pervasive culture of influence, requires fortitude. To demonstrate to skeptics how scrupulous we were, we videotaped every annual lottery and offered to show it to anyone who doubted the integrity of our process. No one ever took us up on this offer to sit through what is arguably the most boring hour of viewing in the annals of media history.

However, as many critics of charter schools have argued, with justification, the lottery process favors families who, if not demographically middle-class, have the kind of middle-class aspirations similar to those of low-income parents of color who, in the past, have been drawn to the parochial schools. These families have more access to information about options for their children, some savvy about how to navigate the system, and the tenacity to stay with the process. Their children have also been poorly served by the public schools and deserve their seats in the charter schools, but in order to balance their presence with the children of lower-income families with less social capital, required some extraordinary measures. In addition to visiting local Head Start centers and churches, we targeted high-rise buildings in the neighborhood and from the top floor down leafleted every apartment, with the intention of stacking the lottery pool with as many poor families as possible.

The result was a population, which over the years has consistently been 75% low-income and 25% middle-income, as measured by eligibility for free and reduced lunch. The challenge then was to find ways to integrate these families of differing incomes, without driving away the middle-class families seeking more homogeneous environments for their children or alienating low-income families fearful of seeing their children relegated to the bottom of the school pecking order.

There are not a lot of examples of schools that successfully serve families of mixed incomes, particularly when middle-income families are in the minority. We have managed to retain those middle-income families and convince them that our commitment to demonstrating the potential of low-income students does not come at the expense of their children. Black middle-class parents are no different from their white counterparts in wanting to gain the maximum academic advantage for their children, which often means shielding them from poor children, who, in their opinion, lower the scholastic bar and distract from instruction with their "bad" behavior. One parent asked me when we were going to get "better" students for our school (read: get rid of the poor kids). My reply was "Never." They were all our children and we were going to do our best to serve, an awkward message for a white administrator to be delivering to a black parent, aware of her own tenuous position in the middle class and fearful of losing her family's toehold on that ladder rung. The painful truth remains, in fact, that virtually all of our graduates who are admitted to Chicago's elite selective admissions high schools come from that middle-class group. The school has succeeded in moving the bulk of our students up to a middle level of performance, but our low-income students haven't yet broken through that glass ceiling.

Almost every new school I'm familiar with follows a rational grow out pattern in which you begin with the earliest grade to be served and adding one grade each year until you reach full capacity. Our situation called for an extra little curlicue. We opened with grades pre-K, kindergarten, 1, and 5, 110 students in all. The addition of the fifth grade was another example of overdetermination. Since the school was designed from the outset to be a "professional development school" serving the other schools in the Center's network, the principals of those schools were eager to have it be a resource to both their primary and upper-grade teachers. If the school followed the conventional path and just grew out from the bottom, it would take years for upper-grade teachers to find in it anything relevant to their work. In addition, the local political leaders, including the alderman, who had been instrumental in overcoming the community's suspicions of the university's intentions in proposing the charter school, were eager to gain as much benefit as possible for their constituents from the school's existence, so expanding the number of available grades was an additional feather in their cap. It was already frustrating to them that the charter law, since somewhat modified, precluded the establishment of neighborhood attendance boundaries, thereby depriving North Kenwood Oakland residents of automatic access. Finally, a slightly larger population base for the school provided a start-up budget that allowed for some modest programmatic bells and whistles that the school needed to get off to a strong start—technology, additional staff positions, and so forth.

However, the decision to include fifth-graders from the start had unintended consequences. Fifth grade is not a common movement grade in a city where most elementary schools are K–8. So, why were families bringing their children to us in this "off year"? For some, it was the cachet of a university-supported school. Whatever its residual reputation as enemy of the community, local folks simultaneously respected the university as a purveyor of quality education. Perhaps some of that might rub off on their kids. This attracted a group of motivated, diligent students who were not being well served by their neighborhood schools. A larger group in that inaugural fifth-grade class was made up of students who were in trouble in their current schools, either for academic or behavioral reasons. They were looking for a second chance. The same was true of our first-graders, another unnatural transition year. We actually received thank-you calls from local principals for taking some of their most troubled charges off their hands.

So this bimodal class of fifth-graders was the vanguard of our new school, the groundbreaking creators of our school culture, for better and worse. That culture, created at the outset of a school's existence, whether by design or by accident, is hard to shake. The pioneer group brought with it many behavioral problems that consumed considerable energy in that first critical year. In many ways, behavior was more of a foreground issue than instruction, which slowed progress toward the learning goals articulated in the school's proposal. These were problems we had no intention of sidestepping. We were not about selectively "good" kids. Our message was to demonstrate that we could be successful with the same population of students not being served well by other schools.

Everything that happened during that first year contributed significantly to the creation of the school's culture that would be with it for years to come. Therefore, it was important to have in place from the outset the proper balance of what the Consortium on Chicago School Research has identified as academic press and high expectations on the one hand, and social support on the other. One manifestation of the academic press and high expectations was our introduction in that first year of an end of year Rites of Passage ceremony. Students were presented with challenging academic projects of writing, reading, and research to undertake. Those who successfully completed them were honored at the Rites of Passage ceremony at the end of the school year. Many of the projects had a distinctive cultural component—studies of African cultures, readings of black authors, research into African American history. This project was the inspiration of one of our veteran black teachers, Lou Bradley, who also served as my mentor on racial issues, those that arose and those that had the potential for arising, and I supported her efforts wholeheartedly. It is essential for white teachers and administrators to seek out mentors like Lou, without whom I would have missed out on this critical opportunity to signal to parents and students that we were demanding the best from our students. No matter how many years we log working in the black community, white staff will never be of that community, nor will we be fully attuned to the nuances and implications of our actions when they are viewed through that racial lens.

The leadership of the Center, which had been visionary enough to propose a charter school and to convince the university of the value of providing support for it, was at the same time not as keenly attuned as they needed to be to the racial context in which the work was being carried out. They approached our work from a traditional liberal colorblind perspective, which advocated for hiring independent of racial considerations and was nervous about what they saw as the Afro-centric nature of our Rites of Passage ceremonies. Foregrounding race was a direct assault on that very liberal colorblindness that was one of the Center's core values. To their credit, the leadership of the Center, confronted repeatedly by the inexorable centrality of race in almost every issue we encountered, from governance to curriculum, grew increasingly more willing to utter the R word and deal with its implications.

Center staff also suffered from not being fully engaged in the day-to-day madness of school life. They were, at times, bewildered by why educational and organizational initiatives were not moving forward as planned. I once heard an interview with a top White House aide to a recent president in which he described the frustration of arriving with a set of grand plans for the new administration and instead spending the bulk of his time putting out brush fires and addressing crises. Ditto for new schools, but the downside of a relationship such as ours with the university was the debilitating nature of having someone constantly looking over your shoulder, and often lacking sufficient sense of the frailty of the mortals who were charged with carrying out the grand design—tired teachers, demanding or unresponsive parents, deeply troubled kids, overwhelmed leaders—all of whom contributed in different ways to a far from perfect school universe. During my years in Mississippi, at the tail end of the period of intense civil rights struggles, movement people sometimes mused over the fact that historians puzzling over the reasons for their actions and decisions would be likely to overlook the fact that they were sometimes simply acting out of bone weariness.

But the university was not our adversary. Nothing could be further from the truth. The school could not have been born without the university, and it could never have accomplished what it has over the years without that support. Although the school operated largely on the public funds it received as part of its per pupil allocation, the university provided support for some of the unique staffing arrangements that were part of the school's structure, as well as for summer planning time and other aspects of the school budget. A large part of the school's fiscal operation was run through the university's existing systems. The reading assessments, which were the cornerstones of our literacy programs in the primary grades, were developed at the Center. In later years, the technology expertise that resided in the Center had a profound impact on every aspect of the school's operation. Nonetheless, there were days along the way when we felt we had traded the bureaucratic master of the CPS central office for that of the university.

From the outset, placing someone like me in the position of director/principal was a huge act of faith on the part of the university. A very large volume could be written about what I didn't know about school leadership. As a result of my inexperience, there was constant scrutiny by the Center. With the university's name so boldly attached to the school, failure was not an option. From the outset, we were under enormous pressure to succeed, just at the point when we needed some safe time to stumble in the dark while we got our legs solidly under us. The university's presence was double-edged. It provided a safety net for an overtaxed and underexperienced school administration at the cost of, at times, undermining the authority of that school-based leadership.

It's hard to call NKO's relationship with the university a partnership. The school was, in effect, a wholly owned subsidiary of the university. But there are other, more limited partnerships that most new schools need to plug the gaps in their ability to offer everything they would like, particularly in the areas of the arts and social support. In the early years of charter schools in Chicago, there were a number of organizations eager to contribute to improving the city's schools, but deeply frustrated by the obstacles the school system placed in their way. These prospective partners included local museums, arts organizations, hospitals, nonprofit groups interested in ensuring a place for specific topics in the curriculum—the Constitution, the Holocaust. Many sought to enhance their status by affiliating with a University of Chicago–sponsored institution, but none sought to profit financially from their work with us, other than by making their grant applications to foundations and government agencies more attractive. From their perspective, charter schools like ours were a gift from the gods. No middleman, no need to call downtown to get permission, no infuriating layers of bureaucracy to pass through to even have your ideas and your offers heard.

Between the time we received our charter approval in December and the time we opened in September, I explored a wide range of possible partnerships that could enrich our program; some were contacts I initiated and some came to me unsolicited. It was overwhelming. It was heady. It became clear as the opening approached that we were in danger of becoming another example of what folks in Chicago came to call Christmas tree schools, from which many ornaments dangled, sometimes clashing with one another. We were forced back on the core question of what kind of school did we want to be and which of these partnerships actually supported that vision. With that in mind, many dropped away, either because they were not essential, were too costly, or too prepackaged and inflexible to adapt themselves to the unique needs of our school. Often, we had to ask whether the partnership added value to the school in proportion to the time it consumed in planning or the instructional time it subtracted from essential areas. There's something to be said early on, and perhaps beyond, for minimizing intrusions and allowing classrooms to develop their own uninterrupted rhythm and flow. In our zeal to add what these attractive partnerships had to offer, we were in danger of losing sight of our academic core.

I'm not intending to document the successful partners who have been with us over the years, but I would like to describe one that, perhaps more than the others, left its stamp on the school in the critical area we discussed earlier of serving a student population of diverse class backgrounds.

Tony Bryk, the visionary director of the Center for Urban School Improvement,[1] had heard a presentation by a group from the University of Wisconsin, which had created a program called FAST—Families and Schools Together—which was designed to build social capital among parents of very different class backgrounds who might otherwise have no occasion to interact with each other. One evening a week for 11 weeks, between 12 and 18 families, parents and children, sat down to dinner together in the school cafeteria. There were rituals and songs reminiscent of summer camp, somewhat embarrassing, but highly effective in creating bonds among the participants. At some point in the evening, the children were shepherded off to another room to play while parents engaged in serious parenting conversation under the direction of program leaders.

In the early years of the school, several cycles of kindergarten and pre-school parents, who were targeted because they would be with the school the longest and could therefore have the greatest impact on the school's culture, passed through the FAST program. The bonds within and across class lines were strong and enduring in ways that sometimes backfired on us. When the children of an early group of FAST parents entered the second grade, they began to share their dissatisfactions with the children's teacher and other aspects of the school's operation, some justified and some fed by the rumors and misinformation that circulated among this tight-knit group. Seven families decided to remove their children from the school en masse, precipitating a great deal of soul searching about how well we were serving all our families and whether we were communicating effectively with them. Nonetheless, the FAST partnership left an enduring and positive mark on NKO in the form of enduring bonds among parents, both within and across class lines.

Despite the FAST success story, there were missteps in the early years that accentuated the class divisions. The school was governed by a board appointed by the university, which included limited parent representation. Parallel to that structure we created a Parent/Teacher/Community Organization, PTCO, which was intended to be an advisory body providing guidance to parent representatives on the board about parent wishes and interests. I had seen numerous situations in the past where organizations like this were hijacked by the middle-class parents—no matter the race—who were, once again, more organization savvy, had heard of Robert's Rules of Order, and were able to silence less experienced parents with that knowledge. Yet, in spite of our awareness of this danger up front, it happened anyway, and, at the expense of considerable animosity, the organization had to be dismantled and reconstituted before it created permanent class divisions among the parents, with the middle class in the ascendance, despite its statistical minority, while poorer parents fell silent and became withdrawn. The trappings of democracy do not a democracy make, and many parents who are wary of organizational politics preferred to demonstrate their commitment to the school by taking on specific tasks, volunteering to paint the halls, to contribute to a potluck, to chaperone a trip, to build a playground. In its later years, the school seems to have arrived at a healthy combination of inclusive organizational activities and a very active volunteering operation, a definite improvement over our early missteps.

New schools fall into several categories in their approach to curriculum: those that are created around an academic program of which the school wishes to be an exemplar; those that begin, not with a curricular focus, but out of a particular social or artistic commitment, a desire to serve a particular community or population; or those with a general desire to offer better instruction than has been available previously to its students. NKO definitely fell more into the first category. We were born out of a commitment to balanced literacy and the assessments that drive it. The Center for School Improvement, our parent body, had been refining its literacy work over a period of almost 10 years before NKO opened its doors, but schools do not live on literacy alone. The first challenge was to find a math curriculum that was as far along in its development as our literacy program.

No new school director is likely to be expert in all areas of the curriculum, so one is inevitably going to have to make choices based on incomplete and sometimes thinly substantiated information. That was the case for my decision about choosing a math curriculum. After lots of reading and perusing materials, I met with the designer of a program, Children's Math Worlds, which purported to be geared especially to the needs of urban children, and decided to adopt it. This was a decision that came back to haunt me because I was turning my back on Everyday Math, the curriculum that had been created right there at the University of Chicago and was winning proponents all over the country. Flying blind, as I was, EM just felt suburban, not what our kids needed.

The problem was that the program I had opted for turned out to be less far along in its development than I had been led to believe. It was good stuff, but it needed a few more years to be as polished as we needed it to be, so after two years, I put my tail between my legs and crawled back to EM, about which I've developed a more sophisticated understanding, despite some lingering doubts about how well it addresses the needs of our students. EM and the other so-called Reform math curricula tend to presuppose that students are grounded in basic math facts and operations, or will arrive at that mastery on their own. This is not the case for most children in urban schools, and that gap must be addressed in the classroom.

Lisa Delpit, in her book *Other People's Children*, has raised similar concerns about the kind of literacy instruction that is the cornerstone of our school, and her words serve as a reminder and a caution to "progressive" educators like me. But I stand firm in my belief that, provided with the proper supports and delivered in culturally relevant ways, these project-based approaches, rich in student choice, are as much a right of poor children and children of color as they are for suburban children. It needn't shy away from the importance of phonics instruction and vocabulary development and it needn't be delivered in a classroom environment in which the lack of discipline could be interpreted by black parents as not caring for their children. For me, NKO was about demonstrating that those practices we have come to consider progressive were not the exclusive domain of the white world.

Starting a new school is an exercise in the art of triage. With all the best intentions in the world, one has to make peace with the fact that not everything will be in place on Day 1, and in some cases the same will be true by

Year 3 or 4 or 5. This is particularly evident in curriculum. We had no clear sense of what our work should look like in science and social studies, other than that it should match our core areas in favoring project-based, problem-solving instruction over textbook learning. Beyond the articulation of that basic principle, every teacher was on her own. This was a welcome invitation for independent action by some teachers, but it was unendurable for others who demanded clearer road maps and, justifiably, resented the additional burden of having to create their own curriculum. When the school was heavily weighted toward the early grades, this was less of a problem because teachers in those grades were encouraged to focus their efforts on literacy and math in any case, so that children would be prepared from third grade on to tackle the material in the content areas.

In my own classroom, I had relished the opportunity to craft my own social studies units. They were delivered with a lot of passion, a commodity in short supply in most classrooms, but in retrospect they were lacking in rigor and devoid of any means of assessing what my students had actually taken away from them. I did have enough good sense to seek out existing curriculum and materials in both science and social studies and adapt them to my needs and interests. However, I was a lone ranger, seeing the world through the narrow lens of my single classroom. New schools require a school-wide vision of how these curricula will build on one another from grade to grade, sedimentary layers, deposited one above the other. Some of this work is still in progress, 14 years past go. We had to learn what every good graduate student knows, that you can't do all the assigned reading for every course with the same degree of thoroughness if you want to make it through intact.

Our core group of veteran teachers carried a lot of curriculum in their heads and taught superbly from that reservoir. The problems arose as the school grew and younger, less experienced teachers arrived and found no road maps to guide them. The 12-month work cycle of those early years was partially intended to allow for documentation of those unwritten curricula, some of which did, in fact, take place, but the exhaustion of a long school year took its toll on people's efficiency and the Center later resorted to bringing in non-teaching staff to help construct those road maps. The process often resembled my efforts to capture my mother's best-kept recipe secrets by following her around the kitchen scribbling furiously about every action on the road to a perfect banana cake. Time is the constant enemy of all good work and mere mortals, wonderful teachers though they may be, are not going to have every tool in their workshop honed and oiled to the same degree right from the start.

And, one final return to the ever-present 800-pound gorilla of race. Like the majority of new schools, ours was started and led by white people serving a population consisting almost entirely of children of color. The suspicion and wariness that disconnect introduces into the start-up process can't be underestimated. To begin with, the University of Chicago, whose name was so prominently attached to our school, was an undeniably white institution with a history that included not just the residential racism we've already recounted, but a record of turning its researchers loose on the surrounding black community in a manner that many saw as exploitive, a one-way street that brought benefits to the researchers, but little to the community. Wasn't the school going to be more of the same, an opportunity to use children of color as experimental guinea pigs? In any free association test, the word *experiment* will, for black people, open wide those doors of mistrust. We had to operate with a keen and respectful awareness of these sensitivities.

On an individual level, I came as the pre-appointed director of NKO, not a choice made by community or parents. As an unknown white presence, there was no way I could avoid being scrutinized through that ever-present racial lens. Early on, rumors circulated that some act of mine—I think it had to do with the lottery, though I can no longer recall the details—was motivated by racism. Fortunately, one of the community leaders who had supported the placement of the school in her domain confronted me with that accusation, allowing me to explain the background behind the decision in question. She was satisfied with my explanation and an issue that could have continued to fester underground indefinitely was, at least for the moment, put to rest.

Similarly, parents who were disgruntled about their child's report card or about the handling of a disciplinary issue by a white teacher sometimes suggested that the problems their child was having were attributable to the white teacher's inability to understand her child's needs, hoping to rouse some support for that position from other parents. My experience suggests that, although race issues are always present, waiting to be voiced in moments of crisis, once parents decide that your actions have demonstrated that you really care about their children and are contributing positively to their education, they are generous in their support and more than willing to move the race questions off the top of their agenda.

Beginning in Year 2 of NKO's existence, the school operated under a co-directorship structure that paired me with a black partner. That cast the racial issue of white leadership of a school serving black families in a different light, but I remained simultaneously grateful for what I was permitted to accomplish by a trusting community in spite of my color and aware of the limitations on those accomplishments imposed by my race. I could never be the model that our black boys so desperately needed, upon whom they could project their own futures. Nor would I ever be capable of exhorting parents and children to higher levels of effort and achievement in any style other than what I always felt was awkwardly white. For the most part, the university and the school leadership had earned parents' trust, but we recognized that that trust could never be taken for granted and re-earning it was a continual process.

By design, the teaching staff was fairly balanced racially from the outset and has remained so throughout the school's 10-year existence. My personal goal, not always shared by the school's sponsors at the Center, was to create an environment, rare in our society, where race issues were always on the table, open for exploration and discussion. Our white teachers were not all equally comfortable talking about race or equally sophisticated about the subtle ways in which it affected their interactions with students and parents. Some insisted on a colorblind stance that failed to recognize that awareness of racial difference was actually a potential asset to their work.

And not all the black teachers fully trusted that their colleagues were capable of teaching other people's children. They questioned the white teachers' management styles as not being informed by a cultural awareness of the approaches to managing behavior favored in black families. They questioned whether white teachers would consistently hold their black students to high standards. They worried about whether the white teachers had the capacity to develop the emotional relationships with black students that those children needed as the bedrock for their willingness to learn.

Recognizing these racial distances among the staff, which rarely manifested themselves in overt friction, led us to incorporate racial conversations as part of our ongoing professional development work. Not everyone welcomed them or saw them as a central part of their mission, preferring to spend that professional development time on increasing their ability to conduct guided reading groups in their classrooms. Still, I remained convinced that it was important to establish this kind of openness around race, both with staff and with parents, as part of the school's commitment to intellectual transparency, provided it promised to enhance the learning of our students, and was not merely an opportunity for racial therapy for the benefit of our staff.

*   *   *   *   *   *

Fast-forward 10 years. We are in the living room of my apartment, the same place where the original teaching staff of the school first met in the months before the school opened. It's been reputed that "All revolutions begin in someone's living room," and ours was no exception. To celebrate the occasion, I have invited the school's pioneers, everyone who was present at the opening, to come together to raise a glass to the infant that has been nurtured and brought to a healthy near-adulthood. The group consists of the teachers, two of whom are still at the school, two classroom assistants who have also continued on, two long-term office staff, the maintenance director, still going strong at the school, beyond his 70th year, the director of operations who left a few years ago to become a classroom teacher, and my first co-director, who in that initial year was not officially on staff at the school, but who was my mentor from the start.

Seated in a circle around my living room, we trade photos, somewhat embellished tales of the memorable kids, both those who inspired us and those who gave us a run for our money, memories of the start-up summer when our inaugural group of fifth-graders, coming from 19 different schools, bonded during a summer of activities at the Field Museum, complete with morning meetings in one of the exhibited tepees, while our church building was being renovated and prepared for our opening.

Several of us return to an image captured in several of the photos resting on my coffee table. Clusters of eager parents gather in front of the church on those first summer mornings to see their children off to the Field Museum for the day's orientation activities. And once again they gather to greet the buses on their return. The photographs bring back the mixture of excitement, anticipation, and anxiety that characterized those days. Parents, whose primary concern was for their children's safety, had entrusted their children to us, and we had returned them whole and, we hoped, enriched, one step closer to becoming a community ready to enter that first school year together.

I am reminded of all the small gestures and activities from the very moment of a school's inception that are laden with implications for community building. Without that attention to community, little of value can be accomplished to advance children's learning, even though they may never be aware of all these precious moments that serve to build the sturdy nest in which wondrous things can hatch.

NOTE

1. Tony Bryk, then the director of the University of Chicago's Center for School Improvement, deserves full credit for much of the innovative design that accounted for the school's success and his political savvy to make it happen. Sara Spurlark and Barbara Williams, both retired CPS principals, were the school's heart and soul in those early years.

REFERENCES

Delpit, L. (1995). *Other people's children*. New York: The New Press.
Freedman, S. (2004, May 16). "Still separate, still unequal." *New York Times Book Review*. May 16, 2004, p. 28.
Hargreaves, A. and Fink, D. (1995). *Sustainable leadership*. New York: Jossey Bass/Wiley.

3

Urban Academy High School

A Place for the True Entrepreneurs of Education?

ANN COOK & PHYLLIS TASHLIK

New York, the acclaimed innovator since the 1970s for anyone interested in small schools, once provided both the vision and the hope for urban education. Not only educators, but foundations and government officials from small and large cities flocked to New York City schools to learn what they could about improving education for students.

What they observed were small professional communities where teachers were committed to creating student-centered environments, curricula that engaged disengaged adolescents, and school structures where teachers assumed responsibility for policy and administration. They noticed a willingness to put everything on the table, including the use of time, space, instruction, and curriculum. They saw kids who were essentially happy—who weren't hostile or trying to undermine the idea of school. They observed that teachers and students had relationships that were close and trusting.

School officials were grateful for these schools because the kids who had caused despair and even fear were off the streets and attending class. All this at a time when the Bronx was burning and traditional schools were emptied out regularly because of false fire alarms and bomb scares. The small schools were serving some of the city's most challenging youngsters, and they attracted staff who saw education as a way to give students with limited experience access to greater opportunities. The decentralization of the late 1960s created a climate that encouraged experimentation and flexibility.

Many of those who founded the early schools—and later became their "teacher directors"—had been influenced by the movements and spirit of the 1960s: young people who had worked in freedom schools in the South and small schools that had sprouted up across the country. They saw the connection between their school and the foundation of a democratic society. The writings of John Dewey were not just an academic exercise.

In contrast, the current small schools movement and the businesspeople and lawyers in charge allude to a "business model" to develop their data-driven, scaled-up systems. The model they have in mind is corporate, but in no way entrepreneurial. Those involved in the early schools were the genuine entrepreneurs—they had ideas and vision, they were risk-takers. They scrounged for funding, materials, and contacts. They started small and were the trailblazers, with no centralized, top-down control. Eventually, the New York City Board of Education had to play catch-up.

When the board got involved, its earliest efforts sanctioned the work that others had begun and that foundations had funded: Lillian Weber's "Corridor Program" at the City College of New York, Community Resources Institute's "Inquiry Demonstration Project" and the Lower East Side Workshop that redesigned classroom space and furniture. Later, District 4's Tony Alvarado was the unusual district superintendent who said yes when teachers came to him with proposals for new small schools. Small schools flourished as parents began exercising choice over their child's school placement. Perhaps the greatest gift that the central bureaucracy gave these new schools was benign neglect—the willingness to let ideas flourish without a great deal of interference and bureaucratic control.

"SMALL SCHOOLS' PREDICAMENT"

Forty years later, with the support of foundations like Gates and Carnegie, small schools have proliferated across the states. However, in many cases, the promoters of these small schools don't understand that "small" is a necessary but not sufficient condition for excellence. The rules by which the new small schools operate and the data-driven "outcomes" established by the bureaucracy have created what Professor Michelle Fine refers to as "big schools in drag" (1994). Teachers are no longer in charge; their expertise and voice have been marginalized, even maligned. The entrepreneurial spirit that characterized many of the earlier initiatives has been suffocated by layers of bureaucratic requirements—for example, lengthy "concept" papers that, in useless detail, describe some abstract notion of a school, totally disconnected from reality—and layers of excessive and high-stakes exams imposed by federal, state, and city governments, which not only harm students but trivialize the curriculum. Rather than a supportive environment promoting risk-taking and responsibility, we now have an environment of intimidation and top-down control.

The new corporate model of Bloomberg and Klein—as well as the New York City Department of Education's (DOE) chief funders like Gates—is so aligned with a high-stakes test ideology that true innovators are not given a chance unless their proposals support the testing model and can be "scaled up" across the system. The small innovations supported by Klein that endured his 7-year administration are only those that build on test data: the bonuses for principals whose schools get higher test scores, the money given to children for taking tests, the rewards for teachers who raise test scores. Klein's earlier efforts, at the beginning of the administration, that were more focused on curriculum (like the Ramp-Up literacy program) have been marginalized. Similarly, the Gates Foundation, which began in 2003 funding the people who were the innovators, has become impatient with results, desiring the equivalent for education of the two vaccines that inoculate against malaria. The Foundation abandoned "small" in favor of "big," and shifted money from the individual innovators who worked in the schools with children to the larger district, New York City's DOE, with its top-heavy supply of lawyers and non-educators.

"LANGUAGE AND POWER"

One disturbing indicator of the current situation is the language employed by the education bureaucrats. A glance at the titles of those in charge provides a glimpse into the Orwellian world that New York City teachers, parents, and kids now must inhabit. School directors are no longer principals; they are CEOs. And above those hundreds of CEOs are scores of other chiefs: a Chief Accountability Officer, Chief Knowledge Officer, Chief Talent Officer, Chief Portfolio Officer, and Chief Equality Officer.

The DOE is proud of its Product Manager for Knowledge Management, Demand Research Manager, Director of Virtual Enterprise, Director of Restructuring and Human Capital, as well as its dozens of Senior Achievement Facilitators, all promoting outcomes. Student work is referred to as a "tool" that can help improve outcomes, and "outcomes" refers only to test score results.

Language has been totally corrupted. Inquiry no longer means a deep investigation of a topic from multiple points of view; it now means categorizing a group of students for data collection. Interim assessment no longer means what teachers do in classrooms to better understand what their students have learned and how to adjust instruction; it now means a series of computer generated multiple-choice tests that a large corporation (in this case, McGraw-Hill) has published, which is then entered into a student's permanent computerized record. Performance assessment no longer means an opportunity to demonstrate learning through multiple means; it now means how you perform on a standardized test. And the "empowerment zone" doesn't really empower at all since the Office of Accountability holds every principal and every teacher responsible for test scores when doling out bonuses, "progress reports," student promotions, and graduation.

TESTING FRENZY

Perhaps the most visible and far-reaching application of test scores is the recently introduced school report card. Modeled on the dubious Florida grading system, 85% of a school's "progress report"—an A–F grade—is based on standardized test scores. Since every Department of Education (DOE) decision and policy is data-driven, everything must be "spreadsheet-able," every child categorized as a 1, 2, 3, or 4—based on his or her test scores—and all learning broken down into measurable "granular" units. Having invested $80 million in a data tracking system, the DOE is now preparing a pilot project to evaluate teachers according to their students' test score results over the objections of the teacher union.

Teachers are valued only for their ability to raise test scores. Instead of professionals, they've become technicians, and their supervisors, technocrats. According to Thomas Kane, a DOE consultant, teachers' ability to raise test scores plateaus after 3 years; hence, there is little point in either professional development or a tenure track (2010). Indeed, step-by-step, DOE policy has encouraged the idea that teaching itself is a stop-gap experience, perhaps a 2- or 3-year job (like the Teach for America schedule) between college and a "real" career.

Children are to be tested at younger and younger ages (pre-K is now the goal). Getting tough with kids is admired more than professional research, so holding kids back in third, fifth, seventh, and eighth grades is now the policy despite overwhelming research of the past 30 years that establishes a clear link between grade retention and dropouts.

Thanks to mayoral control, the New York City school system—the former capital for innovative education—has reintroduced centralization and now has a chancellor who proudly defines education in the narrowest of terms. Intellectual curiosity, originality of thought, persistence in spite of difficult challenges . . . none of these concerned the former chief educator of New York City. In response to queries about what he does define as "success" for urban education, Chancellor Klein wrote in 2007:

We need to look at all the indicators we have—promotion rates, graduation rates, State English and math test results, Regents pass rates, national test results, and even the results of things like Advanced Placement and PSAT exams—to understand how well our students are performing and progressing. Together, these factors paint a complete picture. ("Overheard in New York," 2007, online)

This is the environment in which new small schools find themselves.

THE FOUNDING OF URBAN ACADEMY

Urban Academy straddles the two eras of small schools in New York. Begun in the 1980s, it has managed to survive pretty much intact into the present. Just how it has survived the present obsession with testing is perhaps the central point.

The school began as a professional development program emphasizing inquiry-based education (when inquiry really meant inquiry). Based in 11 New York City high schools, the Inquiry Demonstration Project, as it was called, worked with groups of teachers to help them introduce more depth and intellectual curiosity into their lessons. In time, staff and teachers from several of the Inquiry schools grew frustrated with piecemeal reform and proposed creating a school designed to serve "at-risk" students. Initially, the school worked as a partner with participating large schools serving as one of New York State's BOCES programs where students spend half a day in their home school and half a day in a specialized school.

Within a short time, it became apparent to the superintendent of high schools that while students attended Urban Academy with regularity, most failed to turn up for afternoon classes at their home school. Noting a good thing when she saw it, Superintendent Ballatt did what the board had been doing since the inception of small schools: playing catch-up to the excellent small programs and schools started by innovators across the city. Very quickly, she asked the staff to make Urban Academy a full-day program.

Students who had previously made failing a way of life, or who had simply disappeared from classrooms altogether, found their way to the school. They came from all five boroughs, from a diverse collection of schools ranging from the lowest-performing high schools to selective schools such as the Bronx High School of Science. An eclectic group of would-be dropouts, the students became absorbed in the challenges offered by the school. Those challenges resulted from a combination of factors: first, a commitment by the staff to adopt inquiry as the school's pedagogy and embed it within the courses; second, a linking of that pedagogy to student interest and skill level;

third, assessment determined by curriculum and instruction (not the other way around); and fourth, a strong desire among teachers to create a professional community, an environment in which teachers would make critical decisions about all aspects of the school—the curriculum, schedule, support services, and the mechanism for accountability. The teachers' determination to create such a community fostered trust among staff and allowed them to experiment, invent, and craft a school that worked for both students and faculty.

The board, grateful that these at-risk students could now be accounted for, allowed the staff of Urban Academy to do what the members of the board were smart enough to know they could not: develop trusting relationships with kids who had rarely trusted an adult, much less a teacher, and create innovative ways to challenge and hold students' attention.

Certainly, the school board's creation of an Alternative School Division, 2 years before Urban Academy began, provided a kind of protective infrastructure. Established by schools Chancellor Tony Alvarado, the alternative superintendency was established specifically to circumvent the high school division, known for its rigid and bureaucratic approach to schooling. For these, and perhaps other reasons, the system gave the school time and distance to develop.

Time was on the side of the staff. There were no inhibiting layers of supervisors, high-stakes tests, spreadsheets, or data mongers. Oddly, in this particular instance—nurturance of small schools—the old board, despite its many flaws, mirrored the behavior of more innovative businesses, where committed groups are encouraged (and funded) to take their idea, implement it, and assume both the risk and the responsibility with few top-down rules—a concept touted by the Bloomberg/Klein administration but rarely implemented.

As with any school, it took time for the Urban Academy staff to stabilize, but as the school's professionalism continued to attract bright, committed teachers, the curriculum evolved, standards rose steadily, and students' successes became the norm. The number of students applying to and attending college climbed, even though the mix of kids from every corner of the city remained the same.

CHALLENGES

There were and continue to be challenges, to be sure. School agendas differ fundamentally from those of school district bureaucracies. A school's agenda is, or should be, focused on creating a culture that fosters community, implements practical ways to realize its mission, and concentrates on the growth of individual children. Departments of Education, on the other hand, worry about aggregate data, organized labor, and the political fall-out from system-wide policy decisions. This essential difference in agenda means that schools, whether large or small, need to pay close attention to how district policies might affect their mission and be prepared to resist practices which seem to undermine their efforts. Urban Academy's efforts to create a school where student choice is important—even in the admissions process—is one example of the agenda clash.

From the outset, Urban was determined to serve primarily students whose prior high school experience had been defined by failure and the school designed an admissions policy to maximize a turnaround. Because of their prior experience, most applicants are seeking a different kind of setting from the previously unsuccessful one; so, Urban designed a process that gave students a say in deciding whether or not to come to the school. Applicants first must visit the school, attend classes, and talk to students even before they complete a written portion of the application. The idea is to give applicants a chance to decide whether the school is a good match for them. Applicants are also provided with information about the school's graduation requirements that are based on a system of performance assessments in lieu of exit exams.

Admission is for the beginning of the fall and spring term only—not once the term is under way. Since the school regards participation in classes as an essential aspect of the school's seminar style of teaching, it seemed obvious that if students were admitted once the term was under way, they would have missed a significant part of the term and would fail classes—not a good beginning for students who had already met with failure.

In the school's early days, such practices clashed sharply with district policies. Calls from the central student placement office routinely ignored school input. "We are sending over Juan for admission to Urban now," the call would usually begin (often coming in the middle of the term). And the school's response—delivered many, many times over the first couple of years—was: "No, the student has to visit the school first, then complete the application process. And, no, Juan can't enter classes in the middle of the term; why would you want to have him begin a new experience by failing?"

Initially, the response was an explanation that that was the way it was done "at Central." And our response was a repeated explanation. Back and forth. Over time, insistence gave way to a question: Can you schedule Juan for a visit? To that, the answer was always yes.

Looking back on these episodes, the lesson is clear; schools need a good sense of what they do and why they do it and where a decision or action is related to a school's sense of mission, it shouldn't budge.

Still another example. While No Child Left Behind has introduced sanctions for those subjects not taught by teachers licensed in the subject area, the issue has been argued for years. The assumption is that only those certified in a particular discipline are qualified to teach it: Only those licensed in math can teach even the most basic math, those licensed in physics must teach only physics, not mechanics, and so on. Although the intent has some merit, such a policy ignores logic and common sense. Of course, no one would sanction a practice in which a teacher whose field is French is ordered to teach calculus because there are too few students wanting to take French and no one available to handle the calculus demand. But creating a system-wide policy on this premise is shortsighted, for it robs students of opportunities to learn from teachers talented in subjects other than the one in which they are certified. For example, a teacher may be licensed in social studies since as a young college student they happened to major in history, but her real love is horticulture and she has pursued this interest as an adult, taking many classes and growing many plants over the years. Although not licensed in horticulture (if there ever was such a thing), imagine the courses she could set up for students that would encourage unlimited opportunities for hands-on science experiments, not to mention a passion among some students for something that will give them a lifelong interest.

A standardized policy based solely on licensing requirements limits choices for students—particularly those attending small schools where one ongoing criticism is the limited curricular offerings. As a staff-run school, Urban Academy supports teachers who can offer intellectually challenging courses to students, regardless of the teacher's license. So it is that basic repair and maintenance (applied physics, electricity, carpentry, and all around problem-solving), geography, toy making (an art/physics course), and cooking (taught by a licensed math teacher), human behavior (co-taught by a social studies teacher and chemistry teacher) and string theory (taught by a social studies teacher) have all been offered at the school. Such courses enrich the curriculum, delight students, and provide intellectually challenging opportunities for teachers. And, despite the possibility of challenge from the district office, the school stands prepared to defend its decision and its mission.

THE URBAN CULTURE

Urban Academy's culture is based on a broad vision as well as the supporting particulars. The vision is of an intellectually stimulating environment that nurtures and challenges students and staff. But the particulars are what make that vision possible: teachers who know their students well and in a range of circumstances and conditions including not only classes, but also twice-yearly all-school projects, trips, hanging out, lunch, tutorials, and conferences. Because the teachers work so closely with students, their voice is critical to the school's direction and success. They know the students' reading and writing strengths and weaknesses and work closely with them to support the hard work of revision; they provide discussion-based classes and listen attentively to students' ideas; they know when barriers or breakthroughs have occurred, and learn which books students will read and which they won't; they meet with them in tutorials and conferences and gain an understanding of what motivates them and what doesn't. They meet their parents and speak with their guardians. This, as well as the passion for the subjects they teach, is the stuff of teachers' lives and profession, the tools of their trade. Why would anyone running a school system not want to build on this valuable knowledge?

Nothing is taken for granted at Urban. Each semester, staff members review their use of time and space, the content of the courses and projects they teach, the composition of their tutorials, the effect of technology on the teaching and learning experience. The revision process they require of students is no less demanding for teachers. For example, at the beginning of the fall semester, teachers collaborate on a choice of topic for the school-wide project. They may choose to work individually or team up with a colleague. Project topics have ranged from politics during a mayoral or presidential campaign, to the environment, subways, fashion, architecture, or the nature of community and cultural institutions. Working together, the staff begins the planning process by coming to a consensus on an overarching open-ended question: Do elections matter? How healthy is New York City to live in? What's good for kids? What is a good museum? Once the question has been determined, teachers develop sub-questions of interest to them. For example, for the question "Do Elections Matter?" groups of students were able to focus in smaller project groups on questions such as: What makes a swing state swing? Who's choosing our president? What is the lasting effect of political art?

The project groups continue to meet for 2 and a half to 3 weeks; on occasion, the entire school community convenes to interview someone who could bring a broad perspective to the question being considered. Thus, during the "Do Elections Matter?" project, politicians campaigning for City Council came before the full school to make their pitch and answer student questions. During the project focusing on "What Is a Good Museum?" a panel consisting of teachers and museum curators debated the question: Whose responsibility is it to make a museum visit enjoyable: the museum's or the museum's visitors?

While the fall project is focused on a single question, the spring project draws on the special interests of teacher teams. For several years, five teachers particularly interested in musical theater have joined together to work with students to stage a musical. In 2 weeks, students and staff band together to create the scenery, costumes, and staging for a full musical production—producing, among others, *Cabaret, West Side Story, Two Gentlemen from Verona, Fiddler on the Roof*, and *Guys and Dolls*.

Other clusters of students and staff have joined social action projects (assisting crews undertaking rehab work in post-Katrina New Orleans) and participated in intensive language and cultural studies (living with families in a Guatemalan village). Each project is intended to encourage teachers from different disciplines to work together, to orient new students to the school's culture, and to explore issues and ideas that may not lend themselves so well to semester-long courses. Graduating seniors often talk about "The Project" as a defining aspect of their Urban Academy experience.

During the project, teachers are also designing the courses they will teach during the coming semester. While licensed in the conventional disciplines, Urban Academy teachers design courses that draw on their knowledge and interests while also challenging and engaging students. Courses proposed are reviewed and assessed by the entire staff. This ensures that teachers rethink their classes and revise courses they have already taught and create new courses to offer either in response to student needs and interests or to further explore a strong interest of the teacher's. Immediately after 9/11, for example, two teachers designed a course called "America at War?" that examined the roots of 9/11 and what America's response might be.

CHOICE

Choice plays a central role when students sign up for classes. To obtain English credit, for example, students might have a choice of several literature courses, such as Latin America Literature, The Memoir, The Ghetto Novel, Indefatigable Volubility (a language and vocabulary class), Brothers Karamazov, Writer's Muse, You Call That Funny?, or Urban Anthology. Instead of U.S. History 1 or Global History 2, they would select from such courses as Eyes on the Prize (a history of the civil rights movement), Supreme Law (an analysis of constitutional law), Women Revolutionaries, Populist Movements, Planning New York (focused on Robert Moses), or Slavery and Freedom in the Atlantic World. Within each course as well, students are also offered choices in the papers they write, the topics they research, and in some cases, the books they read. In fact, offering choices to students is probably one of the most effective ways to effect student engagement.

PERFORMANCE ASSESSMENT

Certainly one of the key features of the Urban Academy, and one that the school has fought hardest to preserve, is the use of its performance-based assessment system. Urban Academy is a member of the New York Performance Standards Consortium, the only group of public schools in New York State to obtain a waiver from the Regents tests, a set of five tests required for high school graduation. In lieu of state-prepared tests, students must demonstrate their learning through a series of performance tasks. The tasks include a comparative literary analysis, a research-based social studies paper, an original science experiment, and an application of higher mathematics. In addition, students at Urban Academy must complete performance tasks demonstrating proficiency in art criticism, creative arts, community service, and library skills. An important feature of the performance assessment system is that all students must present their work in oral form through a presentation, a defense, or an in-depth discussion with an external evaluator. This public presentation is in addition to their required written work. Within each of the performance assessment tasks, students have a choice of both the question and the research they would like to pursue.

Although the city and state focus on test/pass outcomes to substantiate their success, Urban Academy and other New York Consortium schools focus on college readiness and persistence. Urban students participated in a research project of Consortium graduates conducted by Martha Foote (2005). Going beyond merely high school graduation rates, Foote looked at the success students were having once they were in college, specifically students' average GPA and the rate at which they return to college for a second year. In both measures, Urban and Consortium students exceeded national norms. The Urban staff firmly believes that the high standards set for the performance assessment tasks has prepared students to be tenacious and motivated. By the time they arrive as freshmen, they have already read and analyzed a series of complex fictional and nonfictional texts, written and revised dozens of formal essays, developed the art of elaborating and extending their ideas in both their writing and speaking, and become emboldened and confident in themselves as students and learners. They are well prepared to succeed in the post–high school world.

DIVERSITY ACROSS THE SCHOOL

One of the missions of the school is to have a diverse community of students. As a transfer school, students from across the city and from a spread of economic and racial and ethnic backgrounds, apply to the school. What makes Urban particularly unique in this diversity is that students are not tracked either by age or skill level. They sit next to each other in class, and because the classes are discussion-based rather than teacher lecture–based, they get a chance to hear what one another have to say about issues that are important to them.. Not infrequently, they find themselves in agreement with students quite different from themselves or in opposition to those whose backgrounds are like their own. Assumptions about one another become less easy to make.

The goals teachers hold for students apply to all—in this case, a respectful and evidence-based dialogue. For them, it may be the first time an African American student shares a classroom discussion with a white student, the first time all students are encouraged and supported to think of themselves as college-bound, the first time a Latina student and white student develop a close friendship, the first time a student who grew up in one of the nation's poorest communities sits at lunchtime with kids who have had the privileges of the middle class.

Inter-age/grade grouping is another key feature of the Urban Academy culture. Every class includes new and veteran students—those who have just arrived at the school and those who have been part of the community for some time. From a practical point of view, such a policy makes obvious sense for a small transfer school, but inter-age/grade grouping also has a significant impact on school culture—applicable to larger and more traditional school settings: Grouping students across age groups and without regard to credit accumulation has a profound effect on the school's sense of community as well as on its instructional focus.

INTER-AGE GROUPING

Inter-age grouping is another key feature of the Urban Academy culture. Students transfer into the school at any level of their high school experience and select classes according to their interests and needs. Thus, one class may include incoming tenth-graders and graduating seniors. Though challenging for the staff, the policy achieves many goals: New students who may be unfamiliar with discussion-based classes are immediately exposed to the culture of the school and observe their peers actively participating in serious discussions, listening closely to what one another have to say, observing students support their statements with evidence from texts, and respecting the right of each student to have his or her voice heard. By making sure all classes are composed of new and veteran students, the school avoids the problem typical of ninth-grade-only classes where an entire classroom consists of students who have just emerged from the sometimes chaotic middle schools and have had little or no opportunity to observe students behaving differently. Mixed classes allow more seasoned student participants to mentor their peers in quite natural ways.

VIGILANCE

While Urban Academy has been successful at sustaining a culture of inquiry and performance assessment, the effort requires constant vigilance. DOE policies call for excessive testing, a focus on narrow indicators of accountability, a reduction in arts-related spending, and a recentralization of decision making. Such policies have the effect of chipping away at the school's culture and requiring the staff and principal to spend valuable time and energy sorting out what principles are critical to defend, which DOE directives can be ignored, and which can be "reframed" so as to protect the school's mission. These strategies have been particularly important in the present test-driven climate.

One glaring example of this dilemma involves the DOE's heavy reliance on data. The data valued by the DOE differ in form, content, and purpose from the data valued by Urban Academy and other performance-assessment schools. Urban Academy, for example, is focused on the teaching and learning that goes on in the classroom and preparing students to survive in college, while the DOE is focused on graduation statistics that would justify its huge investments in testing and data gathering computer programs. Instead of complying with the DOE's computer-based tracking system where students' grades on test-prep material are entered every 6 weeks, Urban Academy responded to requests for data by submitting three volumes of documents that contained extensive evidence of student work, annotated information relating to the school's teacher-designed courses, samples of students' performance assessment tasks, parent surveys, case studies, and statistics on attendance and progression toward proficiency completion. The idea was to provide evidence that there are alternative ways to know students well and better strategies to plot genuine student achievement.

An example of "reframing" DOE requirements occurred in the summer of 2006, when the DOE suddenly launched a required interim assessment policy based on test prep and testing. Urban Academy, along with other Consortium schools, insisted that there were other, more effective ways than tests to document both the work teachers were doing in classrooms and the results of student performance. Responding to the pressures brought by a small group of schools and parents opposed to a one-size-fits-all policy, the DOE added an option to its accountability arsenal, the DYO (Design Your Own) interim assessment.

Despite the lack of central support and almost impossible time restrictions, 90 schools across the city rose to the challenge and produced a variety of assessment strategies that ultimately outperformed Princeton Review and Northwest Evaluation Association, the DOE's contractors. The teachers who designed the DYOs accomplished their success despite being funded at less than two-thirds the amount spent on the DOE's vendors. Dismal results from the DOE's pilot did not, however, deter the DOE from ultimately awarding an $80 million contract to McGraw-Hill to produce interim assessments for all schools across the city. Urban Academy, along with dozens of other schools, continues to opt for its successful but woefully underfunded alternative interim assessment plan.

PROPHETIC WORDS

Urban Academy and other schools "on the fringe" of the current era in education—an era of top-down, systemic change—continue to survive, but the battle is never really won. The entrepreneurial model never gets the full support needed to really shake up the underlying foundation of school systems. The words of Stephen Phillips, former New York City alternative schools superintendent, seem prophetic. As he said back in 1997:

> Even with the alternative schools superintendency, the fortunes of these schools were very much contingent upon who the chief was, and just how sympathetic he was to letting a group of schools operate differently from the rest. Thus, even though the separate office may appear somewhat secure, there has been no institutionalization of the practices that mark our schools: e.g., the empowerment of teachers, the flattened hierarchy, the small size and personalization, the curricular integration, the performance assessment, the reliance on norms in preference to rules. Nor, even more importantly, has there been any institutionalization of the process we introduced for schools coming into being and shaping themselves. (Phillips, 2003, p. 25)

Although we've achieved a proliferation of small schools, the other features that Phillips highlights—the empowerment of teachers, the performance assessment, norms rather than rules—remain an ephemeral goal for New York City and school systems across the state and the country. What will happen next is very much unknown: Will there still be a place for the true entrepreneurs of education? Will the successes for students they've documented ever be accepted as "data"? Will the models they've created ever be more than a peripheral experience in the long haul toward the centralization and corporatization of public schools?

REFERENCES

Fine, M. (1994). *Chartering urban school reform: Reflections on public high schools in the midst of change.* New York: Teachers College Press.

Foote, M. (2005). *The New York performance standards consortium college performance study.* New York: New York Performance Standards Consortium.

Kane, T. (2010, April 15). *Full committee hearing—ESEA reauthorization: Teachers and leaders.* Washington, DC: U.S. Senate Committee on Health, Education, Labor and Pensions.

Overheard in New York. (2007, November 20). *Eduwonkette.* Retrieved from http://eduwonkette2.blogspot.com/2007/11/overheard-in-new-york.html

Phillips, S. (2003). A separate superintendency. In M. Raywid & G. Schmerler (Eds.), *Not so easy going: The policy environments of small urban schools and schools-within-schools* (pp. 23–32). ERIC Clearinghouse on Assessment & Evaluation.

4

Maya Angelou Public Charter School

A Circle of Trust—
The Story of the See Forever School

JAMES FORMAN, JR., & DAVID DOMENICI

In April 1997, we left our jobs as lawyers to start a school for court-involved kids. We had $50,000, donated office space, and lots of energy. We had no staff, site, curriculum, or other funding. But we had a mission—we wanted to create the best school in the country for kids who had been arrested. And we were in a hurry. We knew kids who needed the school—and they needed it right then, not years down the line. Five months later, we opened our doors to 20 kids and a small staff, crammed into a row house in the heart of Washington, DC. This is the story of how we got started.

BACK STORY I:
JAMES FORMAN JR.

"Tell the judge I want a program," pleaded Eddie,[1] "tell him I don't need to be locked up." Eddie was 16 years old, charged with breaking into a house to steal a TV and VCR, and I, a new public defender in Washington, DC, was representing him. Eddie wanted desperately to go home, and he promised to do everything right this time: He would go to school, attend counseling, and pass his drug tests. I believed him. But I wasn't sure the judge would.

Being a good juvenile defender requires learning a lot about your client's childhood, and the more I learned about Eddie's, the more depressed I became. When Eddie was 8, his stepfather began to abuse him physically. At 10, Eddie began to act out in school, fighting with other kids, refusing to do his homework, and eventually repeating two grades in elementary school. Later, he was referred to an "alternative" school, where instead of getting the best of what our school system had to offer, he got the worst. I had been to the school, and it was a place where teachers never assigned homework, nobody talked about college, and kids walked the halls afraid of being jumped.

I had become a public defender so that I could fight for kids like Eddie. My parents were active in the Student Non-violent Coordinating Committee (SNCC), and I knew that their generation had banged down doors so that I could walk through them. For me, that meant Brown University, Yale Law School, and a clerkship for Sandra Day O'Connor. At the same time, I knew that a large part of the African American community had not reaped such rewards. More and more poor blacks were going to prison, not college. Despite the civil rights movement's victories, a black man born in my generation who dropped out of high school was more likely to go to prison than was a black man of my father's generation.

As much as I loved my job, I was constantly frustrated by the lack of good choices for kids like Eddie. The government's only solution was juvenile prison, at a cost of over $50,000 a year. But when I scoured the community for good alternatives to prison, I kept coming up empty. There were not many programs, and those that existed were often low-quality, underresourced, and poorly staffed. As a result, even when I won a case, my clients often returned to the same bad circumstances they were in before I met them. Recidivism was not inevitable, but it was too common.

In Eddie's case, I didn't convince the judge. Eddie was sent to juvenile prison, where he would be held until he was 21 or the Youth Services Agency decided to release him, whichever came first. A few months after Eddie was sent away, I got a call from a friend of a friend. His name was David Domenici, and though I had met him once or twice, I didn't know much beyond the basics: His dad was a U.S. senator, he worked at a corporate law firm, and he did a lot of work with kids. David explained that he wanted to meet to discuss an idea: He was worried about kids who dropped out of school, hung out on the streets, and were assigned to terrible alternative schools. He was thinking about creating a program—a *good* program—for these kids.

BACK STORY II:
DAVID DOMENICI

After graduating from college in 1986, I went to work in New York for an investment bank. A friend and I invited students from Paul Robeson High School in Brooklyn to our offices one afternoon a week. We ostensibly taught them about business and finance—what we really did was get to know them and share cookies and snacks courtesy of Lehman Brothers. Our weekly visits grew into a summer program, in which four students agreed to come to Washington, DC, work part-time, and experience living in a college dorm.

I then decided to attend Stanford Law School, but I didn't want to give up on our summer program. So, along with a small group of my classmates, I helped create a program called DCWorks, in which rising high school seniors spent the summer preparing for college and work. DCWorks targeted low-income, minority students who were doing okay, but who needed a boost if they were to attend college. A perfect candidate would have Bs and Cs—not be a troublemaker, but also not a "star."

During my second summer of law school, I interned at the Public Defender Service (PDS) in Washington, DC, and there I met a whole new set of teens—these were kids who had dropped out of and been kicked out of school, who had all Fs and Ds on their report cards; kids who weren't going to show up at the counselor's office and pick up a flyer about some summer internship program. Kids like Eddie, James's client.

After graduation, I took a job as a corporate lawyer in DC, but I couldn't stop thinking about the teens I had met at PDS. At the suggestion of a mutual friend, I called James to discuss my idea of starting a student-run business and tutoring program for kids who had been arrested. I asked James if he thought his clients would sign up, and if he'd be interested in working together. He said yes to both. After our meeting, I cashed out my 401k plan (from a few years practicing law) and focused on finding a space out of which to run the program.

THE PIZZA SHOP

A few weeks after that meeting, we purchased a small pizza delivery business located between a liquor store and a nail salon on a tough corner of Northwest DC. We presented teens from the court system with the following proposition: Come for 2 hours of afterschool tutoring, after which you'll get to work in the kitchen, learn how to take orders, prepare food, and manage all the finances, marketing, and other operational aspects of a small business.

We had great fun and our students learned all about the pizza delivery business. Kyle, who was 16, closed out the register at night, signed all of our checks, learned Excel, and balanced our books. Students went with us to the warehouse district to pick up food supplies, ran the mixing machine, and made homemade pizza and lasagna. But we quickly realized that the Pizza Shop wasn't the solution we were looking for. The young people we were working with were still stuck in terrible schools (or not attending school at all), and a few hours a day of tutoring and work wasn't going to alter their life trajectories.

Then we were introduced to two prominent attorneys in town, Reid Weingarten and Eric Holder. Former prosecutors, Reid and Eric had always wanted to do something to benefit the young men they had met in the juvenile system. They formed a nonprofit—which they called the See Forever Foundation—and raised about $50,000. But they weren't sure of their next move. In the early part of 1997, we struck a deal. We would use their money to start a school, which we'd open as soon as possible. By April, David had quit his job and James had taken a leave of absence from his.

We decided that we would open a few months later, in September. This meant that we had slightly over 4 months to, among other things, find a building, hire teachers, recruit students, and raise money to make it through the year—not to mention develop a curriculum that would work for our target students. But the decision seemed obvious. We were young, passionate about the mission of serving kids from the juvenile system, and (somewhat self-righteously) convinced that if we didn't do it, nobody else would.

By late August, it was clear that we were going to face some challenges at start-up. We were not sure that we had legal authority to operate a school. We were not a charter school (we would soon apply to become one the following year), and although the head of the District of Columbia Public Schools (DCPS) had personally pledged his support months earlier, we had yet to receive formal confirmation. (Eventually, on August 27, the deputy superintendent of Alternative Education sent a fax stating that there had been a "misunderstanding" and "DCPS would not be able to support our efforts or ensure" that our kids would earn credit. We opened our doors anyway, as an independent, tuition-free, private school.

Finding a site for that first year was difficult. We couldn't secure an agreement with DCPS to use any of their sites, and other buildings that could work for a small school were in short supply. Over the summer, we found a row house in the middle of a residential street that we thought would work; luckily for us, a Neighborhood Legal Services branch had been there before, so we were able to obtain an occupancy permit because of a DC law that allowed us to grandfather in, based on past use of the site for a nonprofit.

Our little building was homey, but its inadequacies quickly manifested themselves. The basement—where we had just installed our newly donated computers—flooded during a downpour shortly before we were scheduled to open. The building didn't have enough room for a designated cafeteria, so the social studies room would have to double as one. Other things also were troublesome—only two bathrooms, no air conditioning (ouch), sparse technology (we would have to rely on Hotmail accounts), and little office space. And although we had raised $300,000, our projected budget for the year was about twice that (we counted on our ability to raise the rest once we were up and running).

Though many things were hard, finding students was easy. We had only one nonnegotiable admissions criterion: A student had to have been arrested. We leafleted the courthouse, spreading the word among judges, prosecutors, probation officers, and public defenders. By mid-August, we had 20 kids who wanted to come, probation officers and parents asking us to start, and judges who said they would not consider the kids truant if they were in our care. So we opened our doors as an independent, tuition-free program—designed for court-involved kids, and funded entirely by grants and individual donations.

OUR STUDENTS

We ended up with a student body that was entirely African American, overwhelmingly low-income, performing at the fifth- or sixth-grade level, despite being 15–17 years old, and had accumulated few high school credits. We were reminded how far behind they were when we reviewed their applications, each of which included the following math problem:

> You have $10.00. You order three slices of pizza. Each slice costs $1.75. How much change do you have after you pay for the three slices? Please show your work. We are interested in seeing how you try to solve the problem.

Of the first 20 students to enroll, about 10 missed this question. Our students' academic transcripts often looked like a bomb had dropped on them. Many were like that of a student named Perry (who would go on to be a star): five Fs, one D, and nearly 100 days missed last year.

Academic struggles were only part of the challenge. Most of our students had seen things that no child should have to witness—friends and relatives shot, parents on drugs, fathers lost to the prison system. As a result, many suffered from depression and exposure to trauma, for which they rarely had received treatment. And our students were not only victims. Some had caused great harm to others, including acts of violence. (Many of our students had committed crimes that are rarely prosecuted in affluent neighborhoods, including drug crimes and minor fights in school; others had done more serious things, but our position was that no offense disqualified a student from admission.)

Many of our students were angry about the hands they had been dealt. Even though they hadn't traveled much, they knew that just across the city other kids—wealthier, and often (but not always) whiter—lived on cleaner streets, with better schools, parks, and libraries, and less hostile police. Working within the context of this anger was one of our central challenges. We adopted the philosophical position of the principal of an all-black school in Atlanta, about whom Sara Lawrence Lightfoot wrote in *The Good High School* (1985), who believed: "Recognize the rigged race but run as hard as you can to win" (p. 47). Yes, we said, this world won't always be just; yes, the police will too often harass and disrespect you; yes, you may even have to be twice as good, or twice as respectful, or twice as prepared. All of us must work to change those conditions, because the race shouldn't be rigged. But while it is, "run as hard as you can to win."

SEARCHING FOR MODELS

Our search for good models to emulate was depressing. When we asked people for examples of good schools serving kids who had been arrested, they typically said, "I don't know of any, that's why you should start one." At the suggestion of some colleagues, we visited the "best" alternative school in Baltimore, and left dismayed. Only a handful of kids were present; when we asked to see the math curriculum, we were told they "focused on the basics." "Job training" consisted of a computer class where students learned keyboarding. Further, the school was located on a remote site, nowhere near where students lived, and not easily accessible by public transportation. The school's hours were 9:00 a.m. to 2:30 p.m.

Charter schools were just beginning to take root in DC and around the country, but it seemed that few people were starting charters that would recruit the kids we wanted to serve. Some told us, "Honestly, it's too late." Others warned that these kids would bring down test scores and make it harder to create good behavioral norms.

Though we could not find specific models, there did seem to be consensus on what was needed. We talked to experts—educators, juvenile justice specialists, judges, public defenders, and social workers. What worked? we asked. For the most part, they agreed—small classes, high expectations, a rigorous curriculum, relevant coursework, and caring relationships. This lined up fairly closely with what kids from the Pizza Shop had told us. Their list had included small classes, a chance to work and make money, counseling, and teachers who were willing to both challenge and support them. And everyone agreed that to be successful, a program would have to be comprehensive.

A COMPREHENSIVE PROGRAM

Our school day went from 9:30 a.m. until 8:00 p.m. Monday through Thursday. On Fridays, we let out early—at 4:30 p.m. School included job training, counseling, afterschool activities, dinner, and tutoring. All of our students had jobs (and got paid)—our Pizza Shop morphed into a catering operation, which our students named Untouchable Taste (this was an example of letting student autonomy go too far; our customers were perplexed by the name, which our students had chosen because, in their view, something really good was "untouchable"). In addition, we built counseling into the school schedule. Each of our students had one session of group counseling a week, and many of them had individual sessions as well, led by a licensed clinical social worker.

We ran afternoon enrichment classes, followed by dinner and an hour of tutoring. Our tutors were all volunteers; staying open so late allowed us to recruit local college students and young professionals who were busy during the day but could spare an hour a week in the evening. We had a lot of kids who really needed someone to help them complete their homework. In addition, we wanted to confront the barriers that separated low-income black students from older, more privileged adults (many of whom—but not all—were white). By the middle of our first year, we had 60 volunteer tutors (fifteen a night, four nights a week) coming to the school for 1 hour a week. Many ended up doing much more than helping kids with their homework— they built strong relationships, became mentors, and came to us with their concerns when students were faltering. A number of our tutors that first year ended up working with their students until graduation 2 to 3 years later; some even continued to support students after they left for college.

HIGH EXPECTATIONS

The importance of high expectations has become something of a cliché in education circles. Who can be against the idea? But this is an example of the chasm separating the juvenile justice and education worlds. While educators increasingly talk about what percentage of students leave high school prepared for success in college, the juvenile justice world speaks of reducing recidivism rates. The juvenile system's low bar for success influences the programs serving court-involved youth. Schools serving these kids often view their task as getting most kids to school each day, keeping fights to a minimum, and finding an occasional kid who can pass the GED test.

We sought to hold ourselves accountable for more, and we made a practice of telling kids and families the first time we met them that "this is your first step toward college, your first step toward a job you enjoy, your first step toward the life you want." Sometimes those meetings took place in the courthouse or the public defender's office, with kids who had recently been released from jail. We received a lot of blank looks in response. Talking about college and the future was so different from what they had been conditioned to hearing that we may as well have been speaking another language.

Of course, one conversation doesn't change anything. To take effect, the message must be repeated, tirelessly and consistently, by every member of the staff, from the principal to the receptionist to the student interns and school volunteers. More than that, the talk must be backed up by specific action.

CURRICULUM AND INSTRUCTION

We used a modified project-based curriculum. We relied heavily on the ideas espoused by the Coalition of Essential Schools—key tenets included studying material in depth (less is more), focusing on relevance, and asking critical questions. We wanted to help students build the habits of mind they would need to be successful at college and in life. At the same time, we knew that many of our kids lacked basic skills, and we didn't think we could address them fully without specific, targeted instruction focused on building up these skills—this was the "modified" part of the curriculum.

For example, we read *Angela's Ashes* and compared African Americans moving north with the Irish coming to America. But we also studied basic geography because most of our students didn't know the 50 states, much less what or where Ireland was. We studied slavery, Reconstruction, and the civil rights movement. We read the *Narrative of the Life of Frederick Douglass*, *Beloved*, and *Selma, Lord, Selma*. And students wrote essays and gave speeches and participated in mock debates. But we also had to teach basic grammar and punctuation. For many students, we had to actually teach them to read (this meant working on basic decoding skills and expanding sight word vocabulary) through intensive tutorials, often using middle and elementary school materials.

We supplemented our curriculum with extended day classes, often taught by volunteers or community partners. These included dance, art, speech and debate, peace and nonviolence workshops, jazz appreciation, digital music production, street law, and yoga. (Although many of these classes worked out great, some were failures, as some volunteers missed class and others could not manage the students.)

Unfortunately, the quality of our curriculum and instruction varied widely during our first year. Our talented and experienced English teacher smoothly turned our broad ideas into daily lessons. But other subjects were more difficult. For example, the original math curriculum, which David wrote, included a 2-week project entitled "Understanding the Black-Scholes: Risk and Reward in the Stock Market." But our math teacher had just graduated from college, had never heard of Black-Scholes, and kept asking David what textbook we were going to use to teach algebra (she eventually grew into a solid instructor and now heads the math department at an Atlanta high school). And we didn't find a social studies teacher until just before the Labor Day weekend.

Although we suffered from spotty instructional quality, it was not because our teachers didn't care enough. Many critics of schools serving low-income students emphasize that many teachers do not believe that poor kids are capable of excelling. This is what some call the *will* problem. We all had the will (i.e., we believed that our kids could achieve at the highest level and that it was our duty as a school to get them there), but we did not—with the same consistency—have the *skill* (i.e., we did not have sufficient mastery of the incredibly complex craft of teaching, especially teaching adolescents who were many years behind grade level). In order to get better we needed a strategy for professional development (we had little PD beyond our 10 days of training in August). As leaders of a start-up school, we had too much on our plate and we did not offer sufficient teacher observation and support. Passion and willingness to work late into the night carried us far that first year, but we were hurt by the lack of a plan to assess and support teachers, and an inability to evaluate and revamp curriculum and instruction based on student performance.

SCHOOL CLIMATE

We opened our doors during a time when the nation was panicking over a rise in juvenile crime, school shootings dominated the news, and zero tolerance policies were in vogue. Especially given the students we served, not a day went by without somebody asking us how we were dealing with school safety. Our students cared about this as much as anyone. On the school's application, we asked students to tell us the best and worst parts of their last school. We were shocked by how many described lack of safety as the thing they liked least about their schools ("too many fights" was the most common single answer). We knew that school safety was a big deal, but the kids we served were typically thought of as the troublemakers. Their applications were a good reminder of how even the "tough" kids crave safety and security.

Yet we had no metal detectors or security officers. We felt that our kids were constantly being reminded that society sees them as threats; our school needed to be one place where they were viewed as scholars. So we tried to create a community based on trust, mutual respect, and nonviolence. We started the year with a week-long, overnight retreat at Trinity University, a local college. (Overnight retreats have remained important to us; we take one in the fall and one in the late spring—but they now are for 2 days, not 7.) One of our first exercises was to break up into small teams and create a school constitution—using magic markers, butcher-block paper, and masking tape, we created the school we all wanted. It would be a school where teachers would "respect students," come "prepared to teach," and "help students for real." A school where students "do their work" and "ask for help if they don't understand something." A school where everyone was responsible for "keeping See Forever a safe and fun place to learn and work together." And that meant "no fighting" and "no weapons." We chose these rules as a group (though we had some non-negotiables—we rejected the student demand for "no homework on Fridays"), and the Rights and Responsibilities we created adorned the school hallways throughout the year.

It was hard to keep up the spirit of that first week (and like all constitutions, ours was broken almost as soon as we created it). But we tried, and school climate and culture was probably the area we got most consistently right in our first year. Students and staff ate meals together. Teachers often stood outside and greeted students when they came in the morning and left in the evening. We stood up for each other. When the police came around after school questioning kids about why they were on the street at 8:00 p.m., the adults reminded the police that our school had just let out, that our kids had had a long day, and that they were headed home. We went to court with kids— and told it straight to their judges. We took their report cards to the hearings and reported directly on student progress (and problems). We drove kids to the doctor's office and got them glasses when they needed them. If students needed a place to stay, staff opened up their own homes and took them in for short periods of time (and eventually we opened up residential homes).

We finished each week with a full-school "circle-up." We talked a lot about the civil rights movement that first year, and we told students we wanted to create "a circle of trust," a phrase used by SNCC in the 1960s. All staff and students gathered in one room, made a big circle, and gave each other shout-outs. The rules were simple. Nothing negative; say something nice, say something sincere, or don't say anything. Kids thanked staff for helping them and congratulated each other for improving their reading or for coming on time every day; staff would shout out kids for working extra hard on an essay or helping to defuse an argument.

FAMILIES

The relationship between schools and families can be complicated, and this was especially true for us. After all, the parents of our students had typically been underserved by the same terrible school system. They lived in neighborhoods that the rest of society had largely abandoned—areas that had been denied economic and infrastructure investment. It was so tempting to give up on them—to think, "Well, if they cared more, this kid would not be so far behind, or so messed up."

Fortunately, we also were reminded of the opposite—of how most of our students had somebody in their lives pulling and praying for them, hoping that they would have a future that is brighter than the odds suggest it will be. One night, more than any other, drove this point home. One of our rituals was a quarterly Family Night, at which students shared their work and received awards. We defined family broadly; we invited parents, grandparents, siblings, probation officers, lawyers, tutors, pretty much anybody who played a role in our students' lives.

About halfway through the year, one mother—Perry's mom, Ms. Randolph—came to us to suggest that at our final Family Night parents should be given the opportunity to speak on behalf of their child. The theme would be "you made me proud, when. . . ." Her reasoning was compelling. She explained that she and Perry had a good relationship when he was young and through elementary school. But in about the eigth grade, Perry had begun a prolonged downward spiral, including skipping school, using marijuana, withdrawing from her, hanging out with kids who were up to no good, and eventually getting arrested. What she summarized in a few minutes was 2 years of agony for her, as she suffered the parental nightmare of feeling like she was losing her child to the streets. During these years, she reflected, she did nothing but yell at Perry. Every day brought another disappointment followed by an interrogation or accusation ("The school called me again, saying you haven't been going!").

More than anything else, Ms. Randolph said, she was just so tired. Tired of yelling, tired of crying, tired of being mad at her son. And now, for the first time in years, things were different. He was going to school, and he said he liked it. Because the hours were so long, he had less time to get into trouble. Now she got calls from the school just to let her know that Perry had written an excellent essay, or intervened when two students began arguing and helped keep it from turning into a fight. (One of our rules was that a student's advisor needed to call every parent in the first week to inform them of something good the student had done.) Perry had even stopped smoking marijuana (mostly). But Ms. Randolph realized that during the bad years she had almost forgotten how to compliment him—she was stuck in a criticism rut and needed help getting out. And she wanted to do it publicly, and encourage other parents and guardians to do the same. And so the parent-led "you made me proud when . . ." Family Night was born. Ms. Randolph went first, other parents followed, and there was not a dry eye in the house.

PROGRESS IS SLOW AND UNSTEADY

In Hollywood, the school savior story always goes something like this: Kid has all sorts of problems; kid meets caring teacher or is admitted to a good school; kid works hard, loves learning, and turns his or her life around. In the Hollywood version, learning gains are quick and dramatic, and kids rarely stumble on their road to success (and when they do falter it is slightly, and for dramatic effect, as the audience knows they will recover). Our experience was rather different.

We had many disappointments that first year, and losing kids was, by far, the hardest part of the job. We wanted to believe that if we worked hard enough, put enough structures in place, loved the kids enough, held them to high enough standards, that they would all make it. But it wasn't to be. We had kids who came to school for a while, said they wanted to change (and, we think, believed it when they said it), but ended up not making it. Their problems were too deep-set, the external forces pushing against them too powerful. Shawn, for example, got arrested for carjacking one weekend, and we lost him for good. Barry dropped out, saying he just couldn't take the hours. Cynthia was arrested and expelled after trying to steal $2,000 by changing the amount of a See Forever check from $20.00 to $2,000.00.

Even the kids who ended up succeeding stumbled along the way.

For example, Darren had dropped out of school in the seventh grade, when he was 13 years old. He showed up at our school at the age of 17. Incredibly talented—in math, with poetry and spoken word, with computers—he took to the school immediately, and after a few months was a top student, and a staff favorite. But one day he just stopped coming. His family's phone was disconnected, his friends didn't hear from him, his probation officer couldn't find him, and we went by his house repeatedly and found no one. Two weeks later, he showed up at school as if nothing had happened. It turns out his mom had been hospitalized and he and his brother had moved in with an aunt in Maryland. After his mom was released, they returned home and he was ready to get back to school. He said this happened regularly (his mom suffered from a degenerative heart disease). Why hadn't he called us? Because this didn't seem like a very big deal to him—he had been drifting in and out of school for years—and he didn't think we'd really care if he took a two-week break. After all, he pointed out, he had returned to school eventually.

Darren got back on track, but as summer approached, he started coming late, often high. We talked about it with him, we sent him home when he showed up high, we tried to get him to go to counseling or treatment. He refused. After he missed much of the summer, we offered him a deal. To stay in the school, he had to move into one of the residential houses, and come to school on time and not high. He agreed. And although we had plenty of other bumps he graduated and went on to college.

He did well his first semester. In mid-winter, he called from the local jail and said he had been arrested for possession of marijuana—he got caught smoking in his dorm room. He ended up on probation, and finished the year. He eventually earned his BA. A remarkable accomplishment, given where he was when we met him—but not quite the Hollywood script.

SELECTING A SCHOOL NAME

In the fall of our first year, we applied to become a public charter school starting the following year—September 1998. As part of this process, we decided to change the name of the school. We wanted our students to be able to go to a school with a more standard name—one that wouldn't raise questions on a transcript or college application. Our kids faced enough scrutiny already, and going to the See Forever School just added to that. In addition, we thought that giving our kids a role in selecting the name of the school would be empowering. So, we decided to have an essay and speech contest. Students were given a list of 20 people; they had to choose one and write an essay about why the school should be named after him or her, and then read their essay aloud at a family night. The prize was straightforward—the winner got to name the school.

In the spring of 2008, 10 students presented their essays to a packed house at the little church next to our school—we used it as a gathering place for Family Nights and other events our first year. Students, family members, and staff got to vote. Two students tied for the best essay and speech—one recommending that the school be named after Malcolm X, and the other after Maya Angelou. We had not thought about what would happen in the case of a tie. We had been fervently—and secretly—hoping that Maya Angelou would be the winner, because she is a close friend of James's family and had agreed to have the school named after her if she prevailed in the contest. After deliberating overnight, we (in this case, James and David) chose Maya Angelou.

A few months later, Sharon, who wrote in favor of Maya Angelou, gave her speech a second time—this time in front of more than 350 people, including Dr. Angelou, at our first annual fundraiser. In making her case for the name, Sharon pointed out that Dr. Angelou "grew up as a poor little girl. She had only her family and her mind. She went through racism as she grew up. Her stepfather raped her. Her mother and father sent her and her brother away when they were young. She had a baby at a young age." She then compared herself and her classmates to Maya Angelou: "Like Dr. Angelou did when she was a child, See Forever students have had a lot of problems, too. We have problems in our neighborhoods, our homes, and inside of ourselves. But like Dr. Angelou, the students of See Forever are using hard work and education to create a new future." She concluded: "We know, and Dr. Angelou knows, that there are people who say we are criminals, drug dealers, and kids who want to make the society a living hell. We know that we will prove those people wrong. The Dr. Maya Angelou Charter School will treat people by the way they carry themselves and not by their history."

Sharon, and many of her classmates from that first year, did prove people wrong. They've grown up to be caring, productive adults who contribute to their community (two of them actually work at one of our schools), and have jobs and livelihoods that they enjoy. Others have struggled—some are marginally employed, others are locked up in adult facilities, and at least one lost his life to violence. This chapter is dedicated to each of them—the original class of the See Forever, our original circle of trust.

EPILOGUE

In the fall of 1998, we opened up as the Maya Angelou Public Charter School, with 50 students. James returned to the Public Defender Service and David stayed on as the school's principal. We moved out of our row house and into a DCPS building. The following year, we purchased and renovated a new site and grew to 70 students. A few years later, we opened a second high school, and then a middle school. And in the spring of 2007—10 years after we quit our jobs to start a school primarily for kids coming out of Oak Hill—we were asked to run the school *inside* Oak Hill (the District's long-term secure facility for adjudicated youth), which we call the Maya Angelou Academy.[2] More than 600 students now attend our schools.

As a part of becoming a public charter school, we could no longer have our special admissions criteria: that all students had to have been arrested. The Maya Angelou Public Charter School campuses are now open to all comers, but remain committed to serving the city's most underserved students. Our public charter high schools are designated as "alternative schools" by the District, meaning that more than 50% of our students are either involved in the juvenile delinquency system, foster care system, have dropped out of school, or were expelled from their previous school.

We've remained best friends. David is at the College of Education at the University of Maryland, and James is now a professor of law at Yale University, and the chairman of our Board of Trustees. Memories of that first year working and learning with Sharon and her classmates continue to sustain us and remind us why this work is valuable and meaningful.

NOTES

1. All names have been changed.
2. We describe this effort in Domenici & Forman, 2011.

REFERENCE

Domenici, D., & Forman, J. Jr. (2011). What it takes to transform a school inside a juvenile justice facility. The story of the Maya Angelou Academy. In N. E. Dowd (Ed.), *Justice for kids: Keeping kids out of the juvenile justice system.* New York: New York University Press.
Lightfoot, S. L. (1985). *The good high school: Portraits of character and culture.* New York: Basic Books.

5

The Met

Educating a Nation One School at a Time?— Just Do It

ELLIOT WASHOR & DENNIS LITTKY

The authors, founders of Big Picture Learning in 1995 and the Met School in 1996, sat down with a tape recorder and reminisced about starting the Metropolitan Regional Career and Technical Center public school district, which has now grown into six Met Schools in Providence and the Big Picture Learning structure that has created 69 schools in 20 U.S. cities, as well as schools in the Netherlands, Australia, Israel, and Canada.

ON YOUR MARK! GET SET! GO! TAKING BOLD STRIDES

ELLIOT WASHOR: What is one of the examples that shows that we were bold and respectful right at the beginning of the process?

DENNIS LITTKY: We said to Peter McWalters (Rhode Island commissioner of education) that yes, we would set up a school, but it wasn't going to be your average school. We had a particular philosophy. This is the way it needed to be, and we were going to involve the community in its development. We made it clear right away that we had something very specific to do.

EW: I can remember that both of us said to the commissioner that we weren't going to build a school for a thousand kids in one building. Instead, we were going to build small schools. We originally thought that our schools were going to be around 60 students.

DL: The school was to be built in Victorian houses all around town, 50 students in each school. Then eventually we would build a gym for these Victorians.

EW: We said we were going to have a school that was small and not tracked. We were going to take all students.

DL: We knew that most high schoolers described high schools as boring, and we were going to do a school where the students were engaged. That was the top goal. We weren't going to keep students in the building; we were going to use the community to help educate our students.

Another example of continuing to be bold: The school had to be passed by the legislature to have a budget. The legislature passes the budget toward the end of June. We knew if we were going to start a school in the fall we needed students, staff, and a building before July 1. Without any okay from anybody, we went out and hired staff, obviously saying we didn't know if you would have a job until July 1. I think there were 40 parents who wanted their children in our school, and there was not even a school passed yet. We did all that work so we wouldn't have to say, "Oh my gosh, we only have a month left and that isn't enough time." So, we began by being bold and saying that we were moving forward. Before we even had a school, we had parents on the steps of the State House demanding that they wanted a school based on the work we had done with them. We were able to get a part of the community excited enough that it wasn't just two guys from out of town.

EW: This leads to one of the other points, which is about starting before everything is completely and totally planned out. We both feel it is a big mistake for a lot of people when they do so much planning that nothing ever gets off the drawing board. They actually think they know what the playbook is going to look like before they have done the school. Doing all of this work was a difficult decision because we didn't even know if it was going to pass the state legislature, but we decided to go for it because the only way to figure it out was to do it. The commissioner said years later, "The most important thing you did was to start."

WE WERE NOT BOLD ALONE

DL: Being bold and respectful connects to Elliot's thoughts about involving the community; one of our great strengths was that we were everywhere in South Providence. We had the community give us tours and ideas about what the buildings should look like. There were hundreds of people involved in our school. To this day, people say how proud they were to be on that original committee. Other people tried to influence them against us;

what they discovered was that we had already spoken to them in a positive way. The fact that the community heard the good news from us first created a good base, rather than a negative reputation.

EW: The first two people we hired were from the community. Remember when we went to that wild community meeting where they called us Tonto and the Lone Ranger?

DL: We went to one of the more radical community groups in town to present our plan. We thought they would all love it and instead they came in yelling and screaming at us saying, "Who are you coming in *here*?" They didn't believe in us, and that is why, lucky for us, we had our community guy come in. He asked us to leave, then he put himself on the line. He said, "I wouldn't have signed up with these guys if I didn't believe in them." The group settled down and then welcomed us, although still skeptical.

EW: This is what we mean by others being bold and respectful as well. Our community worker exhibited both characteristics in that situation and we were building community goodwill into the Big Picture/Met design.

DL: We knew that half our work was to get the city and the community involved; we knew the other half was to get the Rhode Island Department of Education on board. The commissioner was committed but we needed the commitment from the rest of the department, so we assigned every one of our Big Picture people a person in the Department of Education. Our people had to have lunch and meet every week with their point person. Some of us felt that these sessions were not a good use of time—we were all educators, not politicians. But I remember the moment when we realized the whole experience was part of our goal. What we were doing wasn't working on the design; we were getting 20 more people involved in the project.

EW: That leads us to one of our other points: taking us from bold and respectful to being everywhere. Dennis gave a good example of what it means to be everywhere. Not only were we everywhere in the department, but when people said we would never get the number of internships that we wanted, which is a key component of our program design, we went out into the community, into big businesses and small businesses, and created the partnerships we needed to create.

DL: A year of planning all came down to a particular legislative vote. The original budget was for $400,000, but there was an amendment on the floor to take that money from the Met and give it to the other schools. The only way we ended up winning was that a senator convinced his colleagues to withdraw the amendment. If we didn't have the support of that senator, it would have never gotten started, and the reality, as Elliot already stated, is if we didn't get started then, we may never have started.

Also, everybody needs an angel, both financially and politically. We got lucky; Stanley Goldstein, the CEO of CVS, one of the biggest companies in Rhode Island, was really excited about our philosophy. CVS's foundation gave us money each year, which was greatly appreciated and allowed us some flexibility and, more important, the company and its CEO gave us cover. Both of us, along with the commissioner of education and Ted Sizer, who was then a professor of education at Brown University, one of the leading education reformers in the world, and president of the Big Picture board, decided that we should ask Stan, our angel, to become the president of the Met's board. There were state legislators who were against starting a new school like ours. Stan said to them, "I've been giving money to education for over 20 years and this is my favorite project." The next day I got a call from one of our adversaries, who said, "What the hell did you do? I just got a call from the legislature, and they said to back off."

EW: At one time, they wanted us to be in the Armory. The Armory on Cranston Street is huge, the size of three football fields, which is ironic because our school at that time was so small. The Armory was the state's white elephant—it was an abandoned building, and they wanted to put something in it. They had $30 million of state money to redo the building and they said, "Oh this looks perfect," and to them it did. Sometimes politicians just won't listen to educators, community members, and even the Department of Education. But when a CEO says, "No, we are going to have brand-new small schools," that was the last time we heard about the Armory.

DL: Finding an angel is only the first step. We spent a lot of time together discussing the school, the philosophy, and the politics. We had breakfast with Stan most Sundays. Each year, Stan became more and more committed. Fifteen years later, he is still president of the board and our strongest advocate. It's not just about finding somebody; it's about finding somebody and making him part of your team.

WINNING THE RACE WITH STRATEGY

EW: We didn't have money and we didn't have a place to put the school. We were telling parents that we were going to figure it out, and we were telling students that we were going to figure it out, and we did figure it out. We negotiated to put the school in the University of Rhode Island downtown campus, which is also where the Rhode Island Department of Education was located. If we had waited and negotiated for a building, we would have never started a school.

DL: Where do you put your priorities? Yes, we would have liked our own kind of funky building, but under the circumstances that wasn't our priority. Our priority was to find the cleanest, safest place for our students. You have to decide what your priorities are. What are you going to fight for and get 3 years down the line, compared to 1 year down the line?

EW: It took 7 years to build our building, which is the average time to build a facility. My bet is, if we waited 7 years to start, it would have never happened.

DL: Regarding Elliot's statement about doing and planning, not knowing everything as we got going does not mean that we were not prepared. We produced a 100-page document that was our best guess about every question people asked. So if they asked how we were doing buses, we wrote about that. If they asked what a day was like, we wrote about that. Doing this made us think through the issues, even though we knew that the document was only going to get us to the next step and was not the end-all.

BALANCING COMMUNITY VOICE WITH VISION

DL: There are two ways to get community involved. There are some people who go to their community and ask people what they want; then they build around that, which is fantastic. We did it a little differently; we said we have a design, now we need help in how we carry out that design. It's a way to involve the community honestly, without sacrificing the fidelity of what you are doing. I think that's really important because sometimes people who are planning schools get confused. They have strong feelings about what they want, but they leave it all up to the community. They are being dishonest because they really want to do it a different way. It's important to be honest, state what you want, and get the community to help you.

EW: I would say that's one of the biggest mistakes people make. The first thing they do is hold a charrette and brainstorm with the community; they say, "What do you want your schools to look like?" The result much of the time is schools that inevitably look like the schools they themselves went to, with a few little cosmetic changes. When you're talking about fundamentally changing and redesigning schools, you have to stick to your guns.

DL: That doesn't mean that within that context we had strong feelings about, for example, whether students called their teachers Mr. or Mrs. or not; that was not something that was going to make or break the school. We called the whole school community together, and asked, "How do you feel about using teachers' first names?" We would have been willing to go with whatever the vote was. You also have to decide which things are very important to the community. They ended up telling us how they really care about respect . . . if you can get respect by using first names or last names, then it is okay. This is interesting because for a lot of the parents it's disrespectful if you call an elder by the first name, but they went with that. It's being flexible enough within your own philosophy. We also believed that we should start the school at 9:00, when adolescents' brains start working. A similar process took place in which the community agreed that was the best time to begin the school day.

The other thing we decided was that if we were working with a diverse student body, we were going to have a diverse staff. Again, how do you be bold and stay with your goal? We looked at probably 100 people and picked five. The majority of candidates were white, and we had five great white teachers. We actually had eight, then stopped and said we're starting over again, and this time we set a goal: We were going to interview 30 people of color in the next week. We did not lower our standards; we were working hard to find diverse people, and we did it! It's staying with your belief and not going with what's easy—well, we interviewed 100 people and couldn't find a diverse staff. Instead, we stopped and started over again.

BUILDING ENDURANCE . . .
STARTING SLOW AND SMALL

DL: Let's talk about starting small.

EW: Starting small, going slow. It sounds like we went fast, but actually we took a year to plan what to do. To us, starting small meant we would start one student at a time, one grade at a time. We had 50 students. We needed to figure out what to do with a small staff that could sit around a table and work really hard. We tried to get the facilities built; we thought they would be built in 3 years. We should thank a lot of people that it wasn't built in 3 years. That process not only made us do one grade at a time, but one school at a time. We built six small schools in Rhode Island. Through that process we learned how to develop, design, and redesign a system of small schools.

We decided upon two schools and approximately 180 students in a space the size of our first building. But the school felt different, like it was getting a little bit too disorderly. There was something going on with such a large number of kids and adults in that space. We knew we had to shift gears. We got another building built, but it was because of our slowness that we did not really backslide. If we moved faster, taking too many students and teachers, trying to do the professional development, and keeping the culture solid, we might have fallen apart.

DL: Part of our strength was our strong ideas, but we listened well, too. We didn't really know what size it should be originally. Each school was going to be 50 students, as Elliot said. Then we had some trusted friends and educators who told us that was too small. So, we started looking around and reading; we looked at Mr. Gore from Gore-Tex, who built parking lots and factories that had spaces for 100 cars. When a lot was full, he built another factory parking lot. We looked at all kinds of numbers. Elliot's right—it had a certain feel at 180. We settled on 120. Could 180 be good with the right space? Maybe. Could 75? Yes. Are some of our schools different sizes? Yes. That was the process of how we got to the final number.

When you are starting small, design is great, but design doesn't mean anything without great people to carry it out. If we did not hire great people, it wouldn't have worked and people would have thought the Big Picture design was wrong, which would have been due to a lack of proper people, not the design. We worked very hard to get staff that were great on the ground with kids, really believed in the philosophy, and were broad thinkers like us.

EW: We need to say two more things about slow and small. When we talk about slow, most people in the United States who were in education and involved in standardization, talked about getting higher efficiency out of everything. Not that *efficiency* is a bad word, but along with the word, *efficiency*, they talk about acceleration. Learning may be a slow process; it doesn't have to be sped up. Sometimes it can't be sped up. So you have to go slow. The same idea applies to students and adults. It takes time to really understand something. Sometimes you can get it quickly, but a lot of times you are fooling yourself. You really have to get involved. I sometimes say, "Slowness is fundamental to quality." If you go too fast, you are going to sacrifice quality.

Here is one other idea on smallness. When you look at villages and cities, people behave differently in different-sized places, and are subject to different rules of behavior in those spaces. When they enter the city, people don't look at each other. They don't walk down the street and say, "How ya doing?" to every person they meet. You might do that in a village. In a small school, you're not passing papers and memos around; everybody knows each other. If you can't get to the size where everybody knows each other, and you're handling real issues through memos, we think you are in trouble. The smallness involves thinking about the relationships with each and every person in that school.

THE RIGHT KIND OF LEADERS

DL: The next topic is having the right kind of leaders. What happens to many new schools is they have a great energetic leader and staff, then those people burn out, and the school never looks the same. It's a combination of what Elliot said earlier about designing the school with flexibility to get to durability. Half the schools in this country probably go down when the leader leaves. You have to set the school up so that when leaders are leaving, other people can take over. How do you support your staff, and support your leaders, so everyone doesn't burn out? Organizational experts are saying a staff succeeds if the leader takes care of his people; a leader who doesn't backslide, but stays with the philosophy, and keeps fighting for what's right.

EW: I would add, leaders generate systems so they can have other leaders move into the system.

DL: We knew that if we came to the Board of Regents and stated that we wanted six small schools, they would ask, "Why do six small schools?" Come on, they already had an architectural plan for a school that looked big and beautiful. So what we did, and this was part of the strategy, was to go to the state Board of Regents every month and get the okay on a different part of our program. We got them to agree that every student should be in an advisory of 15 kids. We got them to agree that students should do a lot of their work outside of the school. After we got them to agree to everything, we asked why build a big building? They nodded, and asked the same question.

EW: I'd frame it by saying that you have to capture the language and develop your own language. We spent a lot of time, even with our staff, arguing about our language, but we knew if we got the language right, it would put images in people's heads about what this looked like. Dennis is absolutely right—the people who sat around that table building that school all had a conception about the school . . . it's a classroom about 800 square feet, vinyl composite tiles on the floor, cinderblock walls. We don't have classrooms, we have advisories. Well, what's an advisory? It has rugs on the floor. It's got sheetrock walls. We could take that apart differently only because we took the power of understanding of what the function was to create the form.

DL: The other piece that goes with Elliot's flexibility and durability was our difficult fight to get movable walls, which cost two to four times more at that time. You can't move cinderblock. We were hoping to build a structure that could move when the world changes.

EW: What about school funding?

DL: I think the only thing to say about funding is that you need to run your school on the money they give you. You can't count on soft money. Most new schools don't have the proper money, so you constantly need to get a little extra to fund staff development, bus trips, or things to help your people. But you can't be so dependent on soft money that the day it goes away, you fall apart.

EW: We were very fortunate that we also had a very good chief financial officer—that's an important position to fill. As educators, we don't bring certain understandings of budgets. Prior to this, we were used to having a central office cover that. When you have your own place, especially a charter or an autonomous school like The Met, you need to have very competent people who have knowledge, relationships, and connections with the outside world. Our people have done this work in their communities. This gives them the credibility with other financial people.

GOING AGAINST THE GRAIN

DL: In the first year, we were an experiment.

EW: When we started Big Picture, we developed a team. We hired people with specific talents and expertise, and experiences in the work that they were doing. We had a curriculum person, a math person, and a technology person. We hired two community people, and a person who could look solely at LTI [Learning Through Internships, now called Learning Through Interests]. Dennis and I were running around organizing, understanding, doing, learning the politics, raising money, getting the facilities pieces going, and holding the group together. It was probably the most creative time at Big Picture, because we were so focused on making that one school happen. It really was our period of enlightenment.

DL: Yes, I think that year of planning and politics was so interesting. We knew from the get-go that we wanted to implement it. It wasn't just sitting and developing a 135-page book. It was being out there every day making deals and connecting up. It made it really exciting to bring our ideas alive. I think of the first couple of years in the same way—as our most creative—because everything was new, and we met every single day on it.

To go back to bold, you can't be afraid to fire someone. Even if you might have hired your friend or somebody with a great reputation as a teacher, if it is not working, you have to move them out. We had to do that, and we kept doing that until we got it right.

We were committed to doing this for all kids. The reality is that when you start a new school in a town, you usually get the students with the most problems. They either don't want to go or were thrown out of another school. You have to be very careful who your students are. The first 2 years almost sets in stone who your students will be forever. If the feeder schools decide to give you every emotionally disturbed student, then that is what you are known as. If they decide to give you every student with learning disabilities, that is what you are known as. We tried to cast a wide net. There is selective recruiting you can do to make sure you get a diverse group. Most of our students during the first year were youth who had problems. Some had already done ninth grade, and wanted to do ninth grade over again. They didn't want to go to tenth grade, due to having such a bad experience. Others just knew they would get beat up in their new school, or didn't do well.

EW: One of the most important things is to state, "We are done talking, we talked it through." A lot of times staff like to talk their way through something. You can't always talk your way through; sometimes you just have to do it. Sometimes it not only takes a consensus, it also takes leadership. We tell staff that we are going to try it; that's how we will figure it out. We'll keep what works, and change what does not.

BUILDING A SCHOOL CULTURE FROM DAY 1

DL: Next is how to build a special image within the school and in the culture. Part of what we did was ask our students what their friends think of the school; they would say, "It sounds whack and sounds retarded." We had to work hard to get our students to understand why our school was great. That is why, on day one, we said this is a college prep school. It didn't mean AP curriculum. It meant every student here has a chance to go to college— that raised the bar. There was an article in the paper citing the goals of the Brown Medical School in our town; they were the same goals as ours. That helped to raise the bar as well. When our students won a well-publicized stock market contest making the most money (fake money, unfortunately), that was talked about. From day 1, we used publicity to build a culture that made it clear that we were smart.

EW: I think there is one thing we do very, very well. Students have a voice and real serious choices about what they are going to learn. They discover who they are, what they want to be, and what their concerns are. That is very, very important. Without that, I don't think you have the kind of culture students buy into. And they know the difference between real and fake because they quickly get bored with something that is fake. If it is not part of their narrative or their story, then I think they are finished right from the get-go. One of the students had a brilliant little statement about her prior school: "There was no say and no way to get say." She felt very, very differently when she walked into our school.

DL: Most managers and educators will tell you it takes 3 to 5 years to develop a culture. Here is the secret: You can begin to do it drastically on day 1. In 30 seconds, the students know what kind of place it is. On day 1 in our school, we had an opening that we called Pick Me Up that was very different. It didn't look like their school. We had the students listen to each other. We had a student on day 1 say to us, "In all my years at school, I had more voice today than I have had in the last 8 years." You must connect your philosophy and how are you implementing it so that you show yourself as being different; everything you do needs to be different. The same goes for celebrations. Celebrations are a part of culture, politically and socially. We knew we had 4 years until graduation. That is a long time to wait for people to be proud. At the end of year 1, we threw a kind of a graduation. We invited all the parents, the commissioner, the mentors, and the community. It was as big as any of our graduations. We took advantage by not waiting until year 4.

EW: We did the same on years 2 and 3.

DL: There were so many celebrations. On day 1, at the end of the day, we had a video put together showing the kids as a group with great music. It pulled them together. It is constantly celebrating yourself, celebrating the good things you do. When we said every student will have an internship, one of the head men in this town stated we would not get 50 adults to be our mentors. We knew could do it and we got 50. They then said, "Fifty was easy; you will not get 100." Six years later, we have a database of 2,000.

EW: When we had graduates, we went in front of the state legislature. The superintendent of Providence got beat up for 45 minutes over standardized test scores; we were afraid the same thing was going to happen to us. If I remember correctly, they were beating her up because of the seat time for science, which she listed as 43 minutes and she needed 45. We weren't even running formal science classes that even had minutes, but we stuck to our beliefs. We felt that the important data was attendance, which was at 96%; the dropout rate was 4%; and a graduation rate of 95%. Those are figures that the public understood. Instead of cutting our budget, we ended up in a little side conversation started with one of the senators, who said, "How much more money do you need?" Sticking with the high ground, what you believe, having the right data, and changing other people's minds are all very important.

FACING AND EMBRACING THE CHALLENGES OF SCALING UP

DL: Now it is time to answer the hard questions. It is time to have a conversation about things that didn't work and what we learned from those occasions when we tried to scale up. The majority of time when we go into a district, the superintendent is willing to have us as a school. But then, most of the superintendents leave and that becomes a problem. In one district, we had a superintendent who supported us tremendously. I went out to eat with this superintendent, talking about these great plans. Shortly after, he resigned. So, then you have to start over with a new superintendent and sometimes, they push you back in ways that are not good and you lose time.

EW: All that takes time and energy and it is not like these same things didn't happen at the Met. Still, people who are in the work of school start-up businesses think, "Oh, you do one and the next one is easier because you know more and of course, it is much easier than the one that you originally started." Well, that is just not true. They all take time and energy, usually more time and energy than you imagine.

DL: Actually, just yesterday I was speaking with someone who is scaling up programs and who comes from more of the finance/business arena. I realized how differently he was thinking about things than we were. He was talking about the efficiency of setting up partnerships—but sometimes partners do not know how to do this work. Consequently, we do whatever we need to do. Some places we had to go back five times, not efficient, though necessary. Each place is so unique and I think we can get better at figuring out what kind of time can we really put in, what are the best activities to reach our goals.

If we had listened to most people, we would not have gone to the toughest cities. When we first went to one in particular, we were told that the city and school district were in state receivership, and yet we are now in our sixth year of our school with two successful graduating classes. We are a shining star in that city. Our school provides a lot of hope. So, how do you make a decision about going to a place that has a lot of political struggles and takes a lot of time and yet, in the long run, if that city works, the whole state starts looking at it as a beacon, and that opens up more opportunity?

DL: Yes, we could have appeared to be more efficient, better at saying, "We have this much money, this much time, where should we put it?"

EW: There are school developers that start off with cut-offs on reading and math scores for entry. Even if you call yourself a dropout prevention school or a transfer school or an alternative school, if you have a cut off at a sixth- or eighth-grade reading level and 40% of the students in the regular public school system are reading below that grade level, who are you really serving and how do you compare your results? There is the potential for a lot of gaming in the system to prove results on tests. Instead, what we need to say is, "Okay, these are the students whom we have chosen because they have chosen to come to our schools, and these are the students that we are going to stick with." There are not enough school developers who do this. Once you stick with your students, you stick with your schools. Superintendents come and go, board members come and go, yet there are only two places in 9 years where Big Picture is no longer around. One was a district decision based on the costs of small schools. The other one was our decision to leave because of a violation of a contract that we signed with them.

Now, do you run into some lows in the life of a school when a principal leaves, or a few teachers leave, or you run into a budget crisis, or your school is just plain not good enough, not up to your quality? What do you do? Do you drop it, or do you try to get them to have a better-quality school, especially when you think about the commitment that you made to a community and the students and parents and teachers that you are serving? These are real, serious issues about leaving a place. It becomes about how much perseverance and courage you have to say, "Things aren't running well. That is not all right, but we are not going to walk away from it. We are not going to push the students out. We are going to stay with it."

DL: And now in our 15th year, we are looking to develop teams of people from our schools who move around to the schools to go deeper—help them do self-evaluations and evaluations of effectiveness. We are starting to get tougher and say, "This is a good school, but it doesn't really follow our distinguishers."

I think there are two areas that Elliot and I have talked about needing improvement. The school's success is pretty dependent on the principal. We have always known that. If we have great principals, then they will involve the community, help choose the right staff, and push back on any kind of philosophical differences in the district. At the beginning, we did some very intense principal training and then, because the districts lost funding or the right timing for an opening, we caved in on the time it takes to work with a principal. We used to have 1 year of training before the principal went in, and then it was like 6 months of training, and now sometimes it's just a summer. During the school year, we continue to bring our principals together twice a year and provide ongoing support through coaching and peer-to-peer networking across schools. Principal development is an area we will always put an emphasis on to make sure that our people are prepared to lead a school.

LIMITS OF A NETWORK: EVERYTHING IS LOCAL

DL: The other area we always think about is: What is going to keep a school going 25 years down the line? We know the superintendent will change, the principal will change, teachers will change, a few times over. Maybe the school's advisory board fights for a philosophy and we spent some time trying to help principals build up those boards. So, regardless of what happens, e.g., if a principal leaves, the board knows the way. They know they need to go out to advocate or hire a principal who supports the philosophy, someone who will fight for the students. In the public schools, if the principal leaves, the district may find an assistant principal from someplace and put him in. This example makes it important for us to work hard on getting a community board that says, "No, we need somebody that looks at one child at a time," and to keep commitment to Big Picture as part of the selection.

DL: When Elliot and I started, we made a conscious effort not to own the schools. We could have gone in any direction we wanted. We could have chosen charters that we owned. We felt we didn't want to be controlling schools that were 3,000 miles away. Even if Big Picture closed its offices, the schools would continue. They are out there. The district owns them. What we really do is the training and the great part is, they all want the training. That is why they signed up. So, it is a positive network that keeps us going.

The other piece that we learned is selection, selection, and selection. We realized if the person is not the right person, all the training Elliot was referring to doesn't mean much. I think selection is a hard thing, because you are trying to get someone from a town that you don't know. Another thing that we said at the beginning is we were going to try to go into smaller cities, because we felt they were more manageable, and I still think it might be interesting to look at that. I think in one of our big cities, we got lost in the city's bureaucracies.

EW: You try hard not to make rules from exceptions. We have learned that some of the small cities have the same problems and are just as bureaucratic as some of the big cities. How do you develop a scenario, a sense and a feel, as you collect data on our work in both large and small districts? How do you measure sweat equity you put in a place? Some of that commitment has to be to the parents and the community, because they don't leave. Once we have a school there, we are making that commitment. It has got to be that type of commitment in some way and that could get violated if there were certain rules about leaving.

The data cities put out on violence show that out of the four most violent cities in the United States, we are in three of them. Those would be places where other people may not go, and yet for some reason, that is where we ended up. In every one of those places, we have some very, very good schools. It is really difficult to make those types of decisions except as a commitment to your practice and a commitment to the people who are in that community.

DL: It is a big plus that we are also actually running a school. You are so much smarter in helping other people run schools. When others see that we really know what we are doing, that we have been doing it for a long time and we are having particular problems, then they understand that we understand the problems out there. It is always healthy to have your leaders, or somebody who is giving the input to the leaders, to be on the ground, otherwise you are up there saying, "They should be selecting better teachers," but then you know that is a hard thing to do. It has really helped our network to know that we are very good at running our *mother ship* school. We have been here for 14 years, and we have all the problems everyone else has, so it helps us be better on that level of authenticity.

We never wanted to do 10,000 schools. Elliot and I sat in a room and we set a number. We said, "Let's get 100 schools and let's get them to be good," because we were looking for people to spread our philosophy. I've heard that the founder of an organization should never do its scale-up, because we have a certain commitment to something and as the years go on, we see that we cannot control everything. In some ways, all our schools are inspired. We always thought they would all look different according to where they are. This is not lowering our standards. It is being realistic about what you can do. We do have a list of design distinguishers that guide each school, but we never meant to be set up like McDonald's, that you do this exactly in these five ways and you get the meat from all the same places.

EW: I think one of the things that students and staff at our schools deal with is the uncertainties of starting a school and engaging students. Uncertainties about what is going to happen next makes things exciting and challenging in the day-to-day work of teachers and students, and also may be stressful. Many policy planners try to make everything as certain and rule-bound as they possibly can. They go "by the book," but the book is only a good guide and when the uncertainty kicks in and somebody gets sick, somebody has to leave, somebody is doing great, or something goes wrong with a building and all those things start happening at once; if you do not have the wherewithal and the perseverance to deal with all the issues as they arise, you are stuck and you freeze.

If anybody can show me out there that they can take a school model on a piece of paper that has been implemented perfectly, my bet is that it is not a good school. The process has got to be much more engaging, rigorous, and relational, really dealing with problems and concerns as they arise. If school planners are doing that and are struggling, I know that they are trying to achieve a high-quality school.

DL: So all in all, we have had a great 15-year run.

EW: Not only do we have a great network of schools, but now people are looking at using Big Picture philosophies inside their own organizations. We are influencing areas beyond schools. Who knows what is next?

Part II

1999–Present

For the new schools that emerged in the years surrounding the new millennium, the educational terrain was comprised of different sorts of political hiccups, cultural and economic negotiations, as well as advancements from those that the schools in the first section of this volume navigated. As can be seen from schools like El Colegio that opened in Minnesota, the first charter-granting state, charter schools in particular gained greater political support, and with that support came greater financing. Nationally, there has been a rapid and intense exchange of failing public schools for either charters or contract schools. But more important, since 1999, the cultural and geographic landscape of the very neighborhoods and cities in which the new schools have opened have been completely transformed by city governments in order to accommodate different economic and social tastes, or better put, a "new urban economy" (Smith, 2002). Unlike the "housing-centered gentrification" that the schools in the previous section observed, schools like Social Justice and City as Classroom located in Chicago saw a new order of gentrification that converted entire social and geographic topographies. Education policy scholar Pauline Lipman (2005) summarizes the era best when she writes:

> The new wave of gentrification transforms whole landscapes. It includes gentrification "complexes" of consumption, recreation, culture, and public space as well as housing . . . [where] quality schools are key to "space marketing" specific neighborhoods to the middle class. (p. 324)

The result has been that white flight has been reversed and urban populations have shifted dramatically—mainly from Brown to white and poor to a new global professional class. In cities like New York, where once white, wealthy parents wouldn't permit their kids to ride the subway north of 96th Street, those same sons and daughters are trying to outbid each other for million-dollar condominiums built inside formerly condemned brownstones in Harlem and sites of city-neglected housing. Indeed, global cities like Chicago have demolished public housing, and as a consequence, those who once lived in places like Cabrini Green and the Robert Taylor Homes have moved to what Lipman calls the "metroregions" (2005); that is, they have moved to the suburban edges of the city into the little "ticky tacky" boxes (Reynolds, 1968) that white flighters of the 1970s once retreated to in order to get away from the increasing *danger*—i.e., blacks and Latinos—in the city.

With the devastating occurrence of 9/11 in New York City, the nation solidified its will to regulate both its national boundaries and schools. What has surfaced in the aftermath of 9/11 is an always already simmering American xenophobia discharged onto schools like Khalil Gibran International Academy, the first bilingual Muslim school in the country led by a Yemeni American woman. Curricular standards are being "developed," and much of public education rests not on the culture of schools or coalitions of essential schools, but instead on content standards, common assessments, benchmarks and indicators, disaggregated percentiles of proficiency, and the drone of policy acronyms like NCLB (No Child Left Behind) that judge a school's AYP (annual yearly progress), or catchy federal initiatives created to compel public schools to fall in line like Race to the Top.

It goes without saying that the new schools started up within a significantly changed national culture. And despite the challenges of space, place, race, money, and politics, the savvy and fortitude of the founders of these schools very much reflect that which Deborah Meier strongly advises in her chapter that opens this volume: These new leaders for the new schools continue to move farther and faster toward their vision, rather than retreat from it.[1]

New, publicly funded schools neither spring up organically from the ground nor start up in isolation of larger social, political, and economic challenges. What becomes clear in both the preceding and following stories is that mere zeal is not enough to start a school. Through the challenges and the progress of these schools, all of which were and are committed to the concepts of equity, access, voice, and justice for poor kids of color, what we learn is to see and understand the multiple internal and external forces and conditions that new schools have to negotiate as they start up, live, and sometimes close. Inevitably, these forces contain the conflicting political agendas of multiple constituencies that bear down on them; they contain diverging economic interests; and they emerge out of both local and national social histories and political motivations—all of these forces tug at, push down on, poke at, and rattle new schools and their development. Significantly, what we learn from the stories of the new schools is how to develop connections between city, nation, and world, but through the fervent passion of educators trying to make seemingly impossible dreams come true for kids.

NOTE

1. The phrase "new leaders for the new schools" is not meant to refer to the not-for-profit urban principal-training organization New Leaders for New Schools or its fellows.

REFERENCES

Lipman, P. (2005). Educational ethnography and the politics of globalization, war, and resistance. *Anthropology and Education Quarterly, 36*(4), 315–328.

Reynolds, M. (1968). Little boxes. On *Ear to the ground*. U.S.: Smithsonian Folkways Recordings.

Smith, N. (2002). New globalism, new urbanism: Gentrification as global urban strategy. *Antipode, 34*(3), 427–450.

6

El Colegio Charter School

Building El Colegio

DAVID GREENBERG

¡Oye joven! ¿Tú vas a la escuela?

Hey, kid, you go to school? Beginning the fall of 1999, and for the following year, this phrase would become a sort of soundtrack for my life.

It took a 15-minute presentation to the Minnesota Board of Education for El Colegio Charter School to be approved as a small bilingual, arts-focused high school in Minneapolis, Minnesota. Well, of course, it wasn't *that* easy. First, my colleague Carmen Lundberg and I got up the guts to dream up a new school after sitting in on an information session on starting charter schools. We then persuaded artist Armando Gutierrez and arts administrator George Sand to help us start a school that would provide instruction in Spanish and English. Then, we looked for an appropriate sponsor, were rejected by Minneapolis Public Schools, and later accepted by Augsburg College. We built partnerships with organizations and agencies in the Twin Cities from the Walker Art Center to the Minnesota Department of Natural Resources. We planned, researched, met, discussed, wrote, revised, and edited a charter school application for an entire year. Then we presented our application to the Board of Education. After our presentation, one board member interrogated us regarding our bilingual instructional plan. In his view, immigrants needed to learn English and assimilate as quickly as possible like his parents. Despite this member's concern, after a year of rejections and moments of progress, persuasions, and networking, the Minnesota Board of Education unanimously voted to approve the opening of El Colegio.

As founders, Carmen, Armando, George, and I came from different ethnic and class backgrounds, but we had a common purpose. What
made us a strong founding team were our diverse professional strengths.
What helped us to make a strong school were our beliefs in equitable education for Latino students and our commitment to using the arts to create
social and academic relevancy in the lives of youth. I am white and Jewish
from a middle class suburb of Minneapolis. After living in Spain for over
3 years, I returned to graduate school, earned my teaching license, and
began a long-term substitute position at St. Paul's Highland Park High
School in their interdisciplinary arts-integrated program. It was there that
I got my first real teaching job in social studies in the school's Spanish
immersion program.

In 1999, once El Colegio's charter was approved, we received a federal charter school start-up grant for $50,000. I quit my job teaching and
made $30,000 as a full-time employee contracted to El Colegio. George, a
white man in his mid-40s, did not speak Spanish and had little experience
working with Latino youth, but his commitment to arts education and
his strong administrative experience as the director of a statewide arts
integration program helped to provide our team with the organization
it required to recruit, open, and run the school. George pieced together
some consulting work during our opening year, and along with about
$6,000–$7,000 from our start-up funds, he was able to make a living and
commit time to the school.

Armando, a 45-year-old Mexican American from Texas, was an accomplished visual artist, and founder and executive director of the Chicano Latino Art Center and Museum known as CreArte. Through CreArte, which
has since closed, Armando provided a venue for local Latino artists to develop an artistic community and exhibit their work in the Twin Cities. We were
fortunate in that Armando was paid through CreArte. For the first 2 years
that the school was open, CreArte shared El Colegio's facility and it was a
key partner in developing the school and supporting its arts programming.

Carmen, also in her mid-40s and originally from Cuba, was a licensed
Spanish teacher who had worked with me to integrate the arts into the
Spanish immersion program at Highland Park. Carmen's vision for El Colegio was to create a small, safe space able to take students away from city
pressures so that they could focus on learning. Carmen's commitment to
youth and her teaching experience made her a great community front person, and she provided a solid foundation for our teaching staff. The year
before El Colegio opened, Carmen continued working full-time at Highland
Park, which meant she could only provide input into the school after work
and at board meetings. Given her limited time, much of the beginning work
of opening the school was driven by Armando, George, and me.

In order to understand the uniqueness of progressive schools like El Colegio, Aurora Charter School (also one of the first bilingual charters in Minnesota), Avalon, and others started in Minnesota, it is important to understand the educational, economic, and political climate of Minnesota in the 1990s. Minnesota is the birthplace of charter schools. In 1991, the state legislature approved the creation of outcome-based schools with a focus on improved student learning, innovation, and teacher responsibility and accountability. This innovative law was part of a movement in Minnesota to expand options for public school students, which began in the 1970s. The Minnesota legislature enacted a number of progressive education programs starting with the authorization of contract, alternative, and "second chance" schools in the mid-1970s, the Post-Secondary Enrollment Options program, which allowed high school juniors and seniors to attend college at state expense in 1985, and the nation's first statewide inter-district open enrollment program in 1988.

These first charter schools were required to be district-sponsored as well as teacher- and parent-driven. School staff and parents elected boards, a majority of which had to be comprised of licensed teachers employed at the school. The initial law allowed for the creation of only eight such schools, but by 1995, the state expanded that number to 40, allowed public colleges and universities to sponsor a total of up to three schools, and replaced the term *outcomes-based school* with *charter school*. Throughout the 1990s, Minnesota continually evaluated, changed, and improved its charter law. The state lifted the cap on the number of charters in 1997; private as well as public colleges and universities, and later large nonprofit organizations were granted permission to sponsor schools; and revenue streams were added to provide increased funding equity for charters.

The strong economy and the push for educational reform in Minnesota and the United States as a whole also benefited charter schools. In 1994, the federal government authorized the Federal Charter Schools Program, providing start-up funds to implement new charter schools. In Minnesota, the legislature made significant efforts to provide funding equity for charters by giving them access to funding sources previously reserved for traditional districts, including transportation revenue, extra aid for low-income students, and per pupil facilities and start-up aid. These changes, improvements, and the demographic shifts in Minneapolis laid the groundwork for new schools like El Colegio (HACER, 1998). Along with Aurora Charter School, El Colegio was the first Latino-focused bilingual charter school in Minnesota.

The economic growth of the 1990s, Minnesota's strong economy, opportunities for employment and education, and the overall high quality of life in Minnesota drew Latinos (primarily Mexicans) to the Twin Cities. The U.S. Census Bureau estimates that from 1990 to 2000, the Latino population in Minneapolis grew nearly 270%, from 7,900 to 29,175, and given the difficulty of providing reliable estimates of undocumented Latinos, this number is probably low. As Latinos settled in Minneapolis, they began to create businesses, and spaces and institutions that responded to their cultural, religious, and economic needs (HACER, 1998). Through collaborations with community development agencies, Latino entrepreneurs began to transform East Lake Street into a vibrant corridor, which was an artery of South Minneapolis that had long been neglected by the city. Latino families bought or rented houses and set down roots. They transformed neighborhoods, long-dying churches were reborn with Spanish Masses and expanded congregations, and family and friends continued to come to Minneapolis to find a better life. As the Latino population grew in Minneapolis, the traditional school system struggled to respond to the growing need for bilingual staff, culturally sensitive teachers, and more ELL (English Language Learning) classes.

As of September 1999, we had 1 year until the school opened and a long way to go. We had no building, no students, and minimal community engagement. But what we did have was key: an office at Mercado Central. Opened in 1999, the Mercado is a site of multiple, mixed markets and businesses owned and operated by recent immigrants who are predominantly from Mexico. Located on East Lake Street, the Mercado was and continues to be a sign of the growth and influence of Latinos in Minneapolis as well as an indicator of their success. El Colegio hoped to follow in the footsteps of the Mercado.

Each morning during the year before we opened the school, I would enter the Mercado and see shop owners setting out their goods for sale: *botas y ropavaquera* (cowboy boots and denim clothes), *trajes de quinceañeras* (15th birthday dresses), *joyeria* (jewelry), and a myriad of *dulces mexicanos* (Mexican candy). I would hear the Norteña y Ranchera music throughout the space and smell the *pan dulce* (sweet bread) fresh from the oven and the *carne asada* (roast meat) being prepared for the lunch rush. At first, I felt a little like a tourist in a small Mexican town seldom visited by gringos. I was one of the few white people who spent a lot of time in the Mercado, that is, more time than it took to stop in for a taco at lunch. Soon I came to know many of the shop owners and workers. Five days a week for an entire year, I learned about the strengths, hopes, struggles, and challenges of a growing Latino community while working to start a school that would help empower the community's youth.

Centered at Mercado Central during the start-up year, I realize that we missed out on perhaps our greatest development opportunity for this new school in the Latino community. In retrospect, we needed to spend more time explaining the rationale behind this bilingual arts model to the

community, and we needed to share how it could benefit the youth and Latino community as a whole. In addition, in order to open a Latino school
in a Latino community, we needed to get input on the educational needs
and wants of the students and families we were planning to serve. We could
have embraced the community as partners in the creation of the school. We
could have hosted weekly lunches down in the communal seating area of the
Mercado. We could have invited shop owners, mothers, and working youth
to engage in discussions about education in order to give them ownership
and leadership in the development of this new school. While we did make
some connections, we were arguably too bogged down by the overwhelming administrative work required to start a public charter school, and that
stood in the way of us doing the kind of community work that was, indeed,
important to the life of our future school.

*   *   *   *   *   *

As Armando shouted, "*¡Oye joven! ¿Tú vas a la escuela?*" to every young
Latino kid who walked past us during that year before we opened, I learned
what it meant to be the full-time start-up coordinator for El Colegio Charter
School.

In designing El Colegio, Armando, Carmen, George, and I drew on our
diverse personal experiences as students, educators, immigrants, and artists,
and we reflected on what we saw in other progressive schools. As a team,
we saw our opportunity to provide a meaningful high school experience for
students, especially Latinos. We saw that Latino students were marginalized
and not challenged with a relevant curriculum in the larger public schools.
We saw El Colegio as an opportunity to treat students as individuals, to tap
into their unique learning styles, and embed art, culture, and creativity into
the learning process. Our experiences at Highland Park engaging students
in interdisciplinary and arts-based learning showed us that a progressive
approach like this could help students to be successful. But we needed to
convince a Latino community of parents who were unfamiliar with a progressive approach to see the same opportunities we did.

For me, the learning curve was steep: navigating the incorporation of
a nonprofit organization, creating ads for local newspapers, searching for
a building, chairing board meetings, recruiting students, learning about
school finance, holding community meetings, exploring community partnerships. The list was endless, and prioritizing nearly impossible. George,
Armando, and I spent endless hours in our small office at Mercado Central strategizing and visualizing: What type of space should we have? How
would art and culture truly come to life in our school? What approach to
teaching and learning would really be best for our school? I was constantly

pushing my comfort zone. I even attended Catholic Mass in Spanish, and addressed a congregation of 400 or more people from the pulpit. I tried to encourage parents and youth to take a chance on our new school. I felt that the more I learned, the less I knew.

Much of the process early on seemed disconnected from the youth we would serve until 17-year-old David Juarez walked into our office one cold Minnesota afternoon in January. David was a hip-looking teenager with a little peach fuzz on his upper lip, and a confidence about him that was unmistakable. David had heard about El Colegio from a poster at the Mercado. He knocked on our door and said he wanted to learn more about the school. Even then, George, Armando, and I knew this was a defining moment in the development of our new school.

David went to South High, a large public high school not far from the Mercado. Although he should have been a junior, he was behind on credits and would certainly not graduate with his class. He lived with his mom and two brothers, and his mom had two jobs to support the family. She cared about his education and future, but she did not have much time to be involved in his schooling. David was not interested in finding a school where he could earn credits quickly and easily. He wanted school to be meaningful, he wanted to be challenged, and he wanted the opportunity to bring his whole self to school. David grilled us. He wanted to know if we knew what we were doing, and what support we would provide to undocumented students. He asked us questions like how El Colegio would help students like him go to college. How would we support him as a young artist? How did we plan to engage the community? Where was the school going to be located? As the conversation continued, we were not sure if we impressed him, but he sure impressed us. David was a student we needed in our school—that was clear. He understood the model we were developing—personalization, integration of arts and culture, project- and community-driven learning. David took an application, left his phone number with us, and told us that he was very interested in the school and would let us know if he planned to attend.

While David "got" what we were about, in many other instances there was a clear disconnect between what we were creating and what students and families understood as school. The schools that most Latino families knew were very traditional: The teacher stood in front of the classroom with 30 or more students lined up sitting in desks, following instructions, and completing *tareas* (assignments). The notion that students could be active participants and creators of their learning in collaboration with the teacher was not an idea that resonated with them. Additionally, many of the parents wanted their students to integrate into the majority society; they did not see sending their students to a small Latino-based school as a path to integration. They wanted their children to attend "regular" schools.

Although Latino parents did not quickly rally to support El Colegio, our model resonated with many education reformers and middle-class white people. Yet, while many were interested in working at El Colegio, very few were willing to take a chance on sending their children to this new school. So, instead of engaging more deeply with the Latino parents as well as allowing our vision to evolve with their input, we found ourselves communicating more with Latino youth directly, many of whom lived without their parents and liked the idea of having a voice in their education. Our marketing efforts were geared toward youth, and it was the youth to whom we reached out at the Mercado.

Our message was clear yet malleable. As a new school, goal number one was to enroll students, and although we didn't say anything students necessarily wanted to hear, we did cater our message to young people as needed. Our message to David Juarez was "Have a more meaningful high school experience in a unique small school. Be in charge of your learning, engage with your community, and prepare for college." Many of the prospective students who were recent Latino immigrants, mostly young men ages 16–20, came to Minnesota to work. At the same time, they saw the benefit of learning English and they were interested in furthering their education. Our message for these youth was "Come learn English, computers, and skills to help you get better jobs." Yet another message we promoted was for those students who had a history of failure in and disengagement with school. The message to them was "Get personalized attention from teachers you can connect with. Do cool projects in the arts and other areas, and make progress toward graduation."

Without a clear place to call home, enrollment efforts went slowly. A school, more than anything (save for the current movement of online schools), is a place, and it was hard to convince David and other students that El Colegio was the school for them when we didn't know where the school would reside. Our office in the Mercado Central was a critical element in the development of El Colegio; however, a mere eight months before opening, the vital piece of the puzzle that had eluded us was locating an actual school building.

As founders of El Colegio, we each had a separate vision for the school's home. Carmen pictured a school that was like a home, removed from the city, where students could come to grow and learn away from the complexities, challenges, and pressures of their day-to-day city life. George, Armando, and I saw it differently, and this would ultimately lead to an irreparable rift. Although we valued and agreed with many aspects of Carmen's vision, we saw El Colegio's home as within, connected to, and ultimately owned by the community. Our vision was informed and supported by a study that had been published in 1998, two years before we opened the school. The study demonstrated that the growing Latino community in South Minneapolis wanted, among other things, a cultural center (HACER, 1998, p. 56). Based on our own perspectives and this study, Armando, George, and I believed that El Colegio could be more than just a school; it could be an art museum and a center of culture, education, and gathering for and within the growing Latino community of South Minneapolis.

To accomplish making El Colegio into a center for the community, we knew that we could not rent from anyone who was likely to be disconnected from the community and neighborhood. We did not want to send our rent out to the suburbs. We wanted to own and control a building in order to develop equity, capital, and wealth within the Latino community. Three issues stood in our way: One, CreArte neither had the capacity to do a fast capital campaign nor the balance sheet to get banks to finance a building; two, charter schools could not use state funds to directly purchase a building; and three, few buildings in South Minneapolis fit the bill (the strong commercial real estate market of the late 1990s meant a low vacancy rate for the type of large, flexible facility for which we were looking). Despite these financing issues, we began our quest to find the right space for the school.

Time that arguably should have been spent on program and community development was focused on tracking down an ideal space. After a fair amount of time working with a realtor as well as driving around looking for "For Sale" and "For Lease" signs, Minnesota's commitment to progressive education would again help provide the answer to our problems. The state was at the forefront of ongoing legislation to support the success of charters. From their inception, charters had been funded at levels below traditional districts; however, in its interest to push for equitable funding for all students, Minnesota made ongoing changes to address that inequity. The most important change happened in 1996, when the Minnesota legislature adopted the Building Lease Aid Program, which provided approximately $1,500 per student per year for charter schools, and covered up to 90% of eligible lease expenses. This law not only provided charters with significantly more funds to rent facilities, but it also "sent a strong signal to the financial community that charters were an acceptable risk for tax-exempt bonds and other forms of long-term facilities financing" (Schroeder, 2004, p. 27). Because Minnesota law prohibits charter schools from using state funds directly to buy buildings, facilities financing has required the creation of separate nonprofit building companies that actually own the buildings and lease them to the affiliated schools. The schools' lease aid payments are then used to pay rent to the building corporations, which use those funds to pay off the debt. El Colegio was one of the first schools to use lease aid to pay rent to an affiliated building company. Importantly, this practice has come under scrutiny in recent years. In 2010, the Minnesota legislature limited new affiliate building companies and opened the door to direct ownership of facilities by charter schools.

During our challenges of finding and financing a facility, we connected with other people in the charter community who had been through the same struggles and shared our vision. In time, we met John Cairns, a lawyer who helped draft portions of the original charter school law, and Dick Ward, a financial consultant. Cairns and Ward had recently helped two charter schools navigate the process to create a building company and finance the purchase and renovation of a facility through the sale of tax-exempt bonds. Although they assured us that our vision could be a reality, we still needed a building.

In late January 2000, we were led to the building that would ultimately become our home. A CreArte board member led us to El Colegio's current home in South Minneapolis. This board member heard that the local grocery store, a 20,000-square-foot space with ample parking was soon to close and be sold. The site was only 12 blocks from the Mercado Central, on a major bus line, and in a safe and changing neighborhood.

The wheels began to spin as Cairns redrafted the school's articles and bylaws to ensure that they were accurate. We created the El Colegio Charter School Building Company (ECCS) at the direction of Cairns in order to pave the way for purchase of the building. Cairns filed for our 501(c)(3) nonprofit status for both the school and ECCS. Not only did we have a charter school to manage, but as of February 15, 2000, we had a second nonprofit on our hands. ECCS was structured in such a way that El Colegio was the sole member of the organization; thus, the El Colegio board of directors essentially controlled it. For this reason, at our March board meeting, George, Carmen, and I elected Armando to be board chair and signatory for ECCS.

I had been the chair of the board of directors of El Colegio from its inception, but that never really meant much. After all, the board members were just Carmen, Armando, George, and me, and board meetings were really planning, or rather school development meetings. There were no formalities and little attention was paid to legalities. This began to change as we set out on the path to purchase and renovate this 20,000-square-foot grocery store. With the formalization of articles and bylaws and the engagement of lawyers and people in the financial community on the board, we needed to be sure to take formal minutes and track decisions more clearly. While ECCS would be the facilities owner, everything hinged on El Colegio's ability to generate funds to pay the facilities debt. It had become clear to me that we were now more than a school: El Colegio was a nonprofit organization entering a realm in which I had little experience. Now we were tying the future of El Colegio to financial markets of which we had little control or understanding.

The spring of 2000 was a flurry of activity around the building, and although Armando took the lead on many of these items while he was also managing CreArte, the building was the center of much of our work as a team. We needed to negotiate with the owner of the grocery store and with the city of Minneapolis, which would have to be involved in financing the project. Outside consultants were hired with the promise of payments from bond proceeds to do market studies, develop financial pro formas, and complete other documents required for financing. By late March, we had identified an architect and reached a preliminary agreement with the seller. The financing, though, was still a long way off, but John Cairns and Dick Ward set out a timeline for us, and in collaboration with the architect, they assured us that we could get everything done in time to open our school in September 2000.

By April 2000, the city council gave preliminary approval for the issuance of $2.2 million in bonds to finance our building, and in May we negotiated a purchase agreement with the seller that hinged on Minneapolis transferring a $100,000 loan made to the grocery store to ECCS, which it eventually did. This added to the total financing amount, and before we knew it, related bond issuance costs along with the purchase price, related debt, and renovation costs had increased the necessary financing to over $2.5 million. More troublesome than that, we were getting word from Dick Ward that they were having trouble selling the bonds. At that time, these types of bonds were still quite new, and at the end of the day they were still unrated "junk" bonds. The institutional investors and mutual funds that typically buy such bonds were wary of investing in 30-year tax-exempt bonds at a relatively low rate of return, and they were wary of putting their faith in the charter school movement, which was still new and unproven. Like us, the market was on a learning curve, and investors were not quite ready to take the risk.

Despite the increased debt with which El Colegio would be burdened, the people who had invested their time and effort with expectations of payments from the sale of the bonds didn't want to let our dream die, and neither did we. We didn't want to compromise on the quality of the facility either. Our students deserved the best. Therefore, in order to facilitate the sale of the bonds, the term was adjusted from 30 years to 3 and a half years, a large percentage of the bonds were changed from tax exempt to taxable, and interest rates were increased. All this would increase the annual debt service, which would require us to refinance once the bonds were due. Fortunately, a market study showed that we were well positioned to meet those targets, especially if we met enrollment projections, and by May we were beginning to gather significant numbers of interested students and families.

The bond salesmen did their work, Armando worked with the architect on the building designs, and as May turned to June, we continued to enroll students while being anxious that we might never meet our timeline. While this was going on, Carmen began to voice her concerns more strongly: Was this huge, beautiful building necessary? Was this really what we needed in order to provide a good education for our youth in a safe, positive environment? Could we handle the debt service? Tensions arose, but George, Armando, and I pushed forward.

Although facilities were a key issue, we knew we were soon opening a school and needed teachers. In the midst of our focus on finding a home, we also had to work on building a team. During the spring, we placed a number of postings in local papers and colleges. We wanted progressive teachers with skills, cultural competence, and an entrepreneurial spirit. There was no shortage of white teachers who, on paper, fit that bill, but we also wanted a racially diverse, bilingual staff that would reflect our student population.

As we reviewed résumés, we framed our interview questions to get at the key traits for which we were looking. Perhaps the most telling question was one that we continue to use: "Share with us your most challenging cross-cultural experience. Why was it challenging?" Especially for white candidates, this question quickly seemed to get at candidates' attitudes and relationships with students of color, and Latino students in particular. The answer that most struck me in these first interviews came from a white woman who was probably in her 50s. The experience she shared was about a visit she had made to Guatemala for a family vacation. Her great challenge had been the constant tugging on her sleeves by Guatemalan children asking her for money or food. She so wanted to help them all, she related, but had felt powerless to do so. We thought, This was her great cross-cultural challenge?! We were (and remain) committed to the idea that working at El Colegio was a job for dedicated professionals who wanted to empower Latino youth. The job was not one for saviors or cultural tourists, which, unfortunately, this candidate was, and she was but one of many.

After multiple interviews, we finally came upon Cathy Bierly, a white woman who was licensed in life sciences and who, while being new to teaching, had spent years working with youth at YMCA camps. Cathy didn't speak Spanish, but with her professional experience, outstanding recommendations, and commitment to all youth, we knew that she as a woman scientist could serve as a powerful role model for all of our kids, and particularly our Latina students. We also found Grant Boulanger, a recent graduate of the English as Second Language and Spanish graduate licensure program at University of Minnesota, who was, like Cathy, new to the profession, but he had spent years teaching second languages at camps and language schools. Grant understood issues around white privilege and the importance of being both a teacher and learner. He brought resources, connections, a deep understanding of language development, and had a high level of Spanish fluency. Both Cathy and Grant seemed willing to take on the task of opening a school. With Carmen's extensive teaching background and my growing administrative skills, we felt Cathy and Grant would provide a nice blend of enthusiasm, optimism, and diverse professional experiences.

In addition to these hires, we still wanted and needed more Latino staff. While CreArte would bring on board Latino artists, we also needed licensed Latino teachers, but we had little luck finding them. Given our uncertain financial situation, enrollment, and inexperience running a school, as well as our small size, we could neither offer salaries that attracted experienced teachers, nor the incentives that the big districts offered to attract recent graduates of color. The state of Minnesota, however, offered flexibility that provided options to us. Qualified community candidates with special talents or qualifications could fill positions and acquire special permission from the Board of Teaching if no licensed candidate could be found to fill a position. We took advantage of this stipulation and hired Yury Guerra, a highly educated Ecuadorian man with a background in Latin American history and literature. Yury would bring the progressive political ideology and the depth of cultural and historical knowledge that we needed. Finally, our team was taking shape.

As we neared the end of June 2000, less than three months before school was to open, Dick Ward shared that we should have all bonds sold by the end of the month. We talked to John Cairns and set a date to sign off on the documents. As board chair of El Colegio, I would have to sign all the documents along with Armando, the chair of ECCS. Up to that point in my life, the most important things for which my signature had been required were personal checks, validating my passport, or signing a lease on an apartment. When the day came to sign the documents that would allow us to sell the school's bonds, we rode up to the 22nd floor of the highest building in downtown Minneapolis to the offices of Briggs and Morgan, Cairns's law firm. We sat in a huge conference room like those on TV. I felt like I was in another world. I really had no idea what I was signing, but sign I did. Document after document after document, I signed willingly. And it was my signature and those documents that unleashed $2,515,000 that would buy our building, renovate and equip it, pay lawyers and consultants, and help us realize our dream of a new school.

We had overcome one huge obstacle, but as I have come to understand in the building and maintaining of a new school, there are always more to come. Closing the bond deal not only led to the acquisition of El Colegio's home, but it also cost the school one of its founders. The direction El

Colegio had taken was no longer that which Carmen had envisioned, and on July 14, 2000, 7 weeks before school was to start, she resigned. The loss of Carmen was a huge blow to our team, one that I didn't fully appreciate for years. Carmen had the ability to make meaningful connections to students, family, and the community, while also being a master teacher with over 15 years of experience. She and I were the teachers around whom the staff was to be built, and now my colleague, partner, and mentor was gone. Although we did find amazing people after much scrambling, the truth is that we never filled the void left by Carmen, not even to this day.

The weeks leading up to the start of school were hectic. While renovations were moving forward, we weren't able to get into the building until mid-October, and portions of the building wouldn't be ready until early November. We needed a plan, and fast. Enrollment was progressing and as of mid-July, we had nearly 90 students registered. So, our new staff collectively tapped into our community connections, and for the first 6 weeks of school we would make the community our classroom.

Opening day came, and 55 students, grades 9–12, arrived, including David Juarez, the young man at Mercado Central who had questioned us about El Colegio's prospects and potential. David even brought his 17-year-old, eleventh-grade cousin. Overall, the group of students reflected our outreach strategies. Very few were traditional ninth-graders: Our students were recent immigrants who had never attended school in the United States; they were over-aged and under-credited students who did not find success in the traditional system; they were aspiring young artists; and, in general, they were young people looking for a different learning environment. As in any school, some were highly motivated and ready to be full partners in their learning, as was David Juarez, and others were completely disconnected from the idea of school. We were committed to honoring each one of these young people—whatever their motivations—and we were also committed to tapping into each young person's unique style of learning.

The first day of school was not quite the magical day we thought it would be. Not only was the enrollment of 55 students low for what we had planned programmatically, but also our financing was predicated on an enrollment of at least 90. Over the next days and weeks, more students trickled in (and some trickled out, not ready for this type of school), which inched our enrollment toward 70, and was enough to keep us afloat. For the next six weeks, we met daily in the school parking lot and set out from there. We rented three 15-passenger vans, and we held classes and learning activities at the neighboring church, the Minneapolis Institute of Arts, the YMCA camp in nearby Hudson, Wisconsin, and in other sites throughout the city. While our dreams were set on that renovated grocery store as a center for our school, youth, and community, we realized that the community was indeed our classroom. Ironically, the students we recruited with that phrase *"¡Oye joven! ¿Tú vas a la escuela?"* were not entering a school, but creating one with us.

*   *   *   *   *   *

Postscript: September 2010 marked the 10-year anniversary of El Colegio's opening. Those 10 years have been filled with challenges, successes, heartbreaks, and triumphs. We have seen a modest growth of our school in terms of numbers, followed by some decline in those numbers from 65 in 2000 and 95 in 2008 to 85 in 2010. We have graduated more than 100 students, many of whom are the first to graduate high school in their family. Many of our graduates have gone on to local community colleges, larger universities in the United States like University of Chicago, and Universidad Autonoma de Puebla, Mexico, and many have earned scholarships. We even hired one of our graduates, who became a licensed teacher.

With all of this success, we have also seen many students leave our school without graduating for very specific reasons. Often, those who leave do so in order to work to support family, or because they become mothers. Some leave because either they or a member of their family are deported. We have a large percentage of our students fighting the challenges that come with being undocumented in this country: little access to college education or employment, and the accompanying frustrations and motivational challenges. We support and push these students as best as we can. Some overcome the challenges and make it to college. Some don't and drop out of school. And what hurts the most is that some die by suicide or gang violence.

Even though we completely renovated the old grocery store into our school/art center, we very quickly saw our lack of foresight in design. After year 1, we tore down and built new walls to create more spaces to meet our needs. In 2008, we were awarded a $465,000 federal charter school facilities improvement grant to create a full commercial kitchen, a complete science lab to support life science curriculum—five sinks, a greenhouse, and more—and to insulate and improve the comfort of the art space because it's cold here during Minnesota winters!

In our 11th year, we are still a young, yet maturing school. We have moved from a school serving 99% Latino students to one that serves 65% Latinos, along with American Indian, African American, and white students. We continue to serve many recent immigrants as well as students who are significantly behind on credits, students excited by art, and students looking for a small, safe school.

We are taking some time this year to clarify what our school is, who we are best designed to serve, and how we can best meet our mission. We are asking ourselves the hard questions that every school like ours should ask at regular intervals: How can we support our diverse students—recent immigrants, native Minnesotans, Spanish speakers, English speakers, and bilingual students—and provide the education they need to be prepared for college, employment, and community leadership?

REFERENCES

Hispanic Advocacy for Community Empowerment through Research (HACER). (1998, June). *Latino realities: A vibrant community emerges in south Minneapolis.* Minneapolis, MN: HACER Author.

Schroeder, J. (2004, April). *Ripples of innovation: Charter schooling in Minnesota: The nation's first charter school state.* Washington, DC: Progressive Policy Institute.

7

City as Classroom School

In All Cities Geography Is Power

LISA ARRASTÍA

> This is our new world—where there is no distinction between
> political and personal anymore.
> —C.L.R. James[1]

*Don't start a school just because you believe in kids and think they
can probably lead the world better than adults.*

*Don't start a school just because you're a damn good teacher and
think good-teaching-and-socially-relevant-curricula-are-all-that-we-need-
to-make-a-good-school-so-why-in-the-heck-don't-I-start-one?*

*And by jeez heck!—as your granddaddy used to say—Don't move to
Chicago, then three years later start a school when your administrative
experience doesn't include opening and running a school in Chicago.*

*If, a few months before the Twin Towers explode people, ideologies,
and imaginings of a bounded America, you move to Chicago and the
expanse of city that you can see in one single sweep of the eye reminds you
of being a kid growing up on 157th Street in West Harlem during the late
1970s and early 1980s, when 96th Street bisected space, place, and people
in Manhattan . . . if in this landscape you begin to see these sorts of divisions
become more muddled and serve as negotiating points for power . . . if you
notice that these points become like extremities of transactions in which*

poor blacks are exchanged for affluent whites and particular housing, schools, and communities are more easily exchanged for different housing, schools, and far wealthier communities . . . if, when you move to Chicago, you have not yet absorbed these facts both intellectually and politically . . . if you have not yet figured out the topological politics of the city, do not let your heart and dreams sway you to start something that will, that can only be, if you don't heed these warnings, a failure. And do not, for this reason or any other that compels you to ignore the realities of the city and your own capacities, start up that school all by your apparently ill-advised, unwary self.

If you have not yet pieced together all the political interrelations between race, space, money, and schools . . . if you do not have full knowledge and perception of these facts or situations before you start up that school, then don't start it up.

As early as 1995, through political and grassroots organizing, members of the Little Village community on Chicago's Southwest side begin to place pressure on Chicago Public Schools (CPS) to create a high school for their neighborhood. The community is one of the youngest in the city, with 4,000 children of high school age and only one public high school with a capacity for 1,800 students. Twenty-five percent of residents have incomes below $15,000. Only 17% of high school residents have a high school diploma, and 5.5% have college degrees. Farragut Career Academy, Little Village's only local high school, has 55% graduation and 17% dropout rates. Despite a $30 million allocation to build a new high school in Little Village, no construction takes place (Stovall, 2005, p. 4).[2]

But school buildings *are* being built in the city, just not in Little Village. In 1999, a selective enrollment high school, Northside College Prep, is built on Chicago's better-resourced North Side. Only 28% of the school's student body is poor, compared with Farragut's 95%. At Farragut, not even 1% of the students are white, yet a third of the students are at various stages of learning English.

By 2000, Little Village still has no new school in the works and Farragut high school's enrollment swells to 2,182 despite the fact that in four years, Northside College Prep's will barely reach even a thousand. Yet another selective enrollment high school starts up, this time on Chicago's near North side. Under the Chicago Housing Authority's Plan for Transformation (2009),[3] the city's most infamous housing project Cabrini Green is slowly demolished and transformed into something called a mixed-income community. The average income increases, but not for the residents displaced by the destruction of public housing, higher rents, and condos with prices starting at $350,000. Only 37% of students at the near North side's new Payton College Preparatory School are poor and 28% are white, and there are no English language learners.

By 2001, members of Little Village are frustrated. Fourteen residents stage a hunger strike to get a new high school, a good one. They pitch themselves atop a once-promised school site renamed for their purposes Camp Cesar Chavez (Stovall, 2005, p. 4). Nineteen days go by. Finally, CPS capitulates. Little Village doesn't just get a school; they get the most expensive high school ever built in the city: a $63 million high school complex with small schools focusing on social justice; multicultural arts; math, science, and technology; and world languages.

Little Village North Lawndale High School campus opens in 2005, but it's 2001 and while the community awaits construction, it rightfully refuses to stuff any more kids into the sardine can that is Farragut. The district offers Little Village a small, innovative high school model from Big Picture Learning in Rhode Island, where there will be no grades or tests and students will learn according to their interests and passions using internships and projects. The Big Picture high school is an easy fix for impatient families because the school can be housed in an already existing site in the community. But then a kid gets shot in another predominantly Latino neighborhood, Back of the Yards. The city gives Big Picture to Back of the Yards, and leaves Little Village waiting, again. People in Little Village start saying the city gave away the school to try and make up for the shooting and decades of neglect by the mayor.

The news that there won't be a Big Picture school in Little Village comes late in the summer. Mothers of the children who were supposed to attend Big Picture end up scrambling to find schools for their kids with help from Chicago Public Schools. Some of the children meant for Big Picture end up sitting at desks in the hallway of already overcrowded high schools throughout the city.

Enter you, still young, with a lot of Energizer Bunny energy. You've experienced Chicago as a senior administrator at Francis W. Parker School, but never really its quid pro quo politics. You think you know enough to start a school because you've run some really innovative programs for kids in Chicago and California, but in truth nothing has prepared you for the indomitable spirit of ten Latinas; the needs of their children and their community; how alone you will be in the upcoming political battle to start a school, find it a place to live, and then keep it alive without true financial backing and political support. Absolutely nothing in your whole professional career or personal life, note even the fact that you were prepared by one of the nation's leading principal training program, New Leaders for New Schools, and the best leadership coach that anyone could ever ask for, Ellen Reiter, prepares you for this.

Beginning in November 2003, you work collaboratively to open City as Classroom School with a formidable group of Little Village mothers whom you call Las Madres. A couple of years earlier, some of Las Madres had been part of the hunger strike. None of them want their kids at Farragut high school. Every mother wants an educational option for her kids. Almost all of Las Madres have a rising ninth-grader in the family. You become emotionally and politically committed to the mothers and their kids. You want to put into action your belief in good teaching and what you call "street curricula"— education on foot where kids can recognize, record, then respond to the economic, political, and social issues their city faces. So based on your commitment to Las Madres and educational philosophy, you start the school promised to Little Village. It's a little bit Big Picture, and a lot something else.

※   ※   ※   ※   ※   ※

It's opening day. August 2004. About 10 minutes away from Little Village in an old Catholic school building, which is now your school, City as Classroom. A friend's Jarocho band plays. Black students from North Lawndale and the West side listen beside Latino students from Little Village. Some move a hip, but most know it ain't cool to look like you're into this Jarocho ish. Your mom is in the audience lookin' fly as usual. Nervous and excited teachers, four of them, move in and out of their classrooms. The classrooms hold throw rugs, beanbag chairs, Fred Hampton posters, spray paint cans, long tables for deep discussions, and copies of Octavia Butler's *Parable of the Sower*.

Filling the school's largest classroom are your school's board members, local supportive educators, community members, families, and a newspaper reporter. One of your closest friends in Chicago, poet Kevin Coval, is in your office waiting to deliver something he wrote for the school. Two students practice speeches they will read after two Little Village officials speak. The officials, Aristeo and Elias,[4] are two important Latinos. They are community and politically minded men. You know there would be no Jarocho band, no opening day, no City as Classroom School if it hadn't been for these two Chi-Town warriors.

All through the months before school opens, these two political pugilists pick up the reins and make City happen. Your father, dead now, is Cuban, and there's something familiar about these two; Aristeo and Elias tell jokes like . . . are both rough and gentle with you like . . . like dad. So you begin to think that a certain comfort is developing among the three of you.

Aristeo and Elias lead you by the hand through this school start-up process. One politically schools you, Chi-Town style. The other makes sure that the political abilities of the community are not forgotten. The whole start-up process has more to do with political meetings, talks with CPS, and charter school groups than it does with finding funding, developing a board of directors, designing the curriculum, hiring teachers and an administrative staff, community engagement, and enrollment.

Aristeo and Elias see before you do how much you don't know.

You don't know that it is smart politics that will get your school open, not the educational ideas that make up a good school. These men are beguiling, and it is because of this that they have gained so much for the 22nd ward and the Latino community on the Southwest side of Chicago. You remain prudent and attentive to potential problems and dangers with the two while simultaneously handing them your gullibility, because you want the school so badly. You just can't face Las Madres and tell them, "Sorry, still no school for your kids." What you do to reconcile your ambivalence regarding the two is you try never to overstep your bounds with them even when they engage in a sort of enticing raillery with you. You let them know you can take it, but something on which you can't put your finger keeps a piece of your trust in reserve.

With the help of Las Madres' protest methods, Aristeo and Elias coax— actually, they halfway threaten—CPS with something like another hunger strike if City as Classroom School does not open. They make deals with other men from the district office in a sort of political dialect with which you are unfamiliar. You are present at the meetings between all of these men, and as all of these men exchange metaphoric handshakes through words you don't really understand the essential parts of a good school that are being surrendered. Then after one of the last meetings Aristeo turns to you and says, "You got a school."

CPS permits City as Classroom to open, but only under the already crowded umbrella of Infinity Charter, a local charter school, and only in Infinity's congested education and training center for Latino immigrants located on the far edge of the Southwest side.[5] It's only later that you realize what really happened in that final meeting at CPS. Chicago Public Schools made Aristeo and Elias an offer they couldn't refuse, but it was a proposition impossible to realize. And perhaps that was the strategy: make City too difficult to open, and if it does open, too weak to survive.

More deal-making ensues as Aristeo and Elias officially ask Nettie Mayes, the executive director of Infinity, to take City under its wing. She knows she has to since the request comes through Elias and Aristeo but down from CPS. No matter, negotiations must be made. Once again, you are amazed at the rate of transfer and weighted elements of political exchange in this semiotics of fast bargains and covenants. But you remain silent and let the makeshift buying and selling of pacts over schools, property, and business between Elias, Aristeo, and Nettie proceed. They all know that you have no idea how to engage in business conventions of this kind, and yes, they take advantage of that. But they do have some confidence that you can lead a school, because you come to them known as a good creative educator. Most important to them is your obvious commitment to the Latinos and African American kids who will attend City.

So after Nettie says something to you like, "Gurrl, you look like you're on the verge of boxer's brain. How long you been in Chicago anyway?" and "Do you know the kind of men you're dealing with?" with a somewhat sympathetic ear she agrees to take on City as Classroom School, but only for one year. With the hairy eyeball she warns, "Don't let me regret this."

Don't start a school when a wise person from a smooth-running organization tells you that a seemingly polite handshake could draw back a nub.

Infinity is a godsend. Pappy Rollins, its chief of staff, is brilliant. He has written the equivalent of an NCLB instruction manual, or better a defiance manual for the organization's principals to help them navigate NCLB's convoluted, unfinanced mandates while not sacrificing the educational innovation and support kids need. Pappy speaks openly with you about educational and political tensions in Chicago. He warns you to distrust the educational arm of the Civic Committee of the Commercial Club of Chicago, which is entrenched in new school start ups. They'll "rape ya," Pappy declares. "If you shake hands with 'em, you'll draw back a nub."

NCLB manual in two hands, you slide down the wall of Infinity. "What have I gone and done?" you wonder aloud. Pappy responds through a snigger, "You done started a school in Chicago."

You have no idea then that Pappy's inconsiderate and inappropriate statement is in some ways accurate. In the city's larger drive toward economic and local geopolitical power, your educational objectives and your school will be treated with irreverence, your trust will be stolen, and your ambition sedated. Of course, it will be nothing like a physical rape. But there will be moments when you are terrified. You will work 7-day weeks on less than 4 hours of sleep. You will be alone in the school all day for 3 weeks with 48 kids, and some teachers out sick, some fired, some just plain gone. You will have one part-time staff person, and you will foresee no way to reverse the scarcity of services in your school. So yes, you will be traumatized, and it will take you several years to emotionally recover from the political stomping and precarious go-it-alone entrepreneurship you're about to experience.

*Don't labor on with a school if you have zero funding from the state
beyond per pupil tuition.*

Being under Infinity means great support in deciphering educational
policy and negotiating its potential impact on the life of the school, but it
doesn't mean the school gets any more money beyond the per pupil tuition
of $5,373, which the state allots during the 2004–2005 academic year. In
reality, Infinity is paid a substantial cut of your tuition, which you negotiate
down, but still weakens your budget significantly. Until you gain charter
start-up funds, you can't enact the full City as Classroom model, you can't
hire a full-time administrative anything, and you can't buy all the supplies
the school needs without continuing to supplement the budget with your
personal credit card. So City's staff is one principal, one quarter-time security person, one part-time administrative assistant, and three teachers until
one wretched day they become just one.

After the deals with CPS and the local charter school are done, there's
one more deal to be finalized with the Latino education and training center
that Infinity runs. The center needs to agree to provide you with some space
to house your school. How you'll pay for this space is a whole other question with which Aristeo, Elias, and Infinity are not concerned.

*Don't start a school if the district only consents to its opening after
it has already laid out the most it's ever paid to build a high school for
the very same politically active community on which the media has just
focused, and your school is intended to serve. That is, don't start up if
support of your school is really just reluctant acquiescence to or maybe
fearful anticipation of loud, publicized community pressure.*

CPS is adamant that the center serve as the school's facility. Amid the
center's half-dozen other community education programs, it houses an alternative high school. You visit the site and meet with the center's president, who
is a good person running an important community agency. But the space is
plop in the middle of an industrial islet and isolated out on a wide thorough-
fare. The center is tiny and overcrowded. Although it's clean, one can see the
weight of the organization's programs taking its toll on the building.

It is hard to imagine your little ninth-graders trekking across a highway,
or faring well against the center's 17-year-old and older supposedly in reform Two-Six gang members who attend its high school. Word has it that
City as Classroom's faculty will have to escort City students to the bath-
room in order to make sure that gang recruitment stays at a low.

Another deal is cut and the president of the center tells you reluctantly,
"I'll share some space," and just as reluctantly you accept. Then the president tells you that City's school day can't begin until after 11:00 in the

morning. City can't have any administrative office space. City can't use the telephone and will have to rely on cell phones. City can't have lunch at a lunch hour that isn't breakfast or close to the end of the school day, and City can't have lunch in the cafeteria but will have to eat outside—even in the winter, in Chicago. City can't store any books or supplies. City can't use the copy machine whenever needed because resources are already slim and what if overuse breaks it? And finally, City can't use the classrooms during most of the day every day. After this litany of can'ts, there is one thing that City can have most of the day at the center, something it can call home base: an approximately 300-square-foot corner of the center's cafeteria.

And you still don't back out.

It's like everyone from CPS on down is just doing Las Madres and you a favor. But a school can't be a favor doled out and exchanged among political foes and friends. Once you understand that the people who have been leading you through this start-up process are less concerned with and knowledgeable about what a school really needs—like classrooms, desks, phones, books, and safety—that's when you set out to find your school a real place to live.

You look at buying in Little Village. Too expensive. Especially because you don't have donors and the board members you're signing on, who are genuinely committed, don't have any real money, just good will and major skills. You look at renting in Little Village, but the topography there is tight.

You call Aristeo. You let him know there is no way that you can have the school start up in the center. He admits, "It's not perfect." He hooks you up with Ernesto, who owns a space in Little Village that is just a bit bigger than your 800-square-foot condo in the West Loop. Ernesto wants to charge you something like $1,500–$2,000 a month plus utilities. When you question "But where do I put the kids?" Ernesto asks, "Well, how many are there?" You tell him by 2010 there'll be 240 students. He says, "We can make it work."

After months of searching, you surrender. You yield to the fact that Little Village is densely populated and space is just plain scarce. What little space is available is overpriced, and there's nothing you can do about it.[6] You tell Aristeo and Elias that the search is drawing up nothing. "Have any other ideas?" you ask them. But they don't. In fact, help from the two has been coming less and less as City's opening day approaches.

It's like a month before the school is supposed to open and the only space you've got is the center's cafeteria corner. A teacher from Francis W. Parker School on the North side where you used to work mentions City as Classroom to the second largest real estate developer in a nearby Latino neighborhood. For some reason, George Doyle is interested in City, finds you, and tells you to come to his office right away. Within hours your desperate butt is in George's dirty office. It's a ramshackle place that has old feces stains in the toilet. He takes you to see some of his properties and you think, *Yikes! This dude's a slumlord*. But you're desperate. Underneath the slumminess, you hope maybe you can find a heart, a donor, and a site for your school. George does have a big heart and he helps, but his help is encased in business and money.

George becomes the chair of City's board, and what you think is a $10,000 donation from him is actually a loan. George finds City a building near his office and furniture. He even offers up his grungy little office in which you can interview prospective teachers and hold meetings until your site is up and ready.

George has done well. The new site is absolutely perfect, at least start-up-charters-facing-facility-challenges kind of perfect. Twenty-eight thousand-square feet of space. Brightly colored classrooms. Two floors for your small school that will begin with 45 ninth-graders, then expand each year. There's a bus stop around the corner, a parking lot, a playground on site, a nearby Mexican café and restaurant, and a corner store where the kids can, unfortunately, buy their daily dose of hot chips.[7] But best of all, what this place has is a cheap lease. Only about $2,000 per month including utilities for the entire building. You believe that with the potential this space offers, Las Madres will have a real school for their children. There's also room to grow in this site located in an adjacent but still Latino neighborhood.

This is exactly where your naïve little self went very, very wrong. You never really understood that in all cities, geography is power, and power is in the geographies of a city.

> *Don't start a school in a city that the 1959 Civil Rights Commission dubbed the most segregated in the nation—a city whose own newspaper still considers it the most segregated even 49 years later (Ahmed & Little, 2008).*

Place matters in Chicago where there are more than 200 neighborhoods. In Chicago, place and power partner in communities for the acclaim and capital that resources like schools, housing, and businesses can bring. Neighborhoods in Chicago are their own micro-nations, each with its own race—mainly white, Latino, or black; each with its own ruler, or alderman; and each with its individual relationship, whether good or bad, to the central authority of the city, the mayor.

All of this—your search for a suitable place in which to locate the school, the covenants you saw contracted and to which you, through your silence, agreed—is like background, faded history once it's opening day, August 2004, and you and City as Classroom School are about 10 minutes away from Little Village in an old Catholic school building in a Latino neighborhood with brightly colored classrooms, your mom in the audience lookin' fly as usual, two students practicing speeches they're nervous to deliver right after Aristeo and Elias deliver theirs.

The Jarocho band is still playing and it's already 9:30 in the morning, but Aristeo and Elias are nowhere in sight.

The phone call to Aristeo goes something like this:

"It's 9:30. You were supposed to be speaking now. Where are you?"

"I'm not coming."

You ask, "What do you mean you're not coming?! Are you sick?"

"Nah, I'm not sick. You knew the minute you moved that school out of Little Village I couldn't support it anymore."

"No, actually, I didn't know that. That's why I'm calling to find out where you are."

You're sweating, long peninsula-shaped pit stains are forming on your dress. You can't hear the Jarocho music, you can't hear the crowd down the hall, just pure silence. Aristeo inserts himself into the silence and says, "You could've kept the school right here in Little Village. We found you a place at the center. But you chose to move the school. So I'm not coming."

You argue that the school is only 10 minutes from Little Village: "How can 10 minutes matter?" But in Chicago, 10 minutes does matter. To gangs and community leaders, space matters.

"You knew this was going to happen the minute you moved the school. Don't act like it's a surprise." But you're not acting. It is a surprise.

"That school was supposed to be for the children of Little Village."

"The school is still for Little Village kids. All of our Latino students live in Little Village. You and CPS knew that the center was unmanageable."

"Yeah, but the school still would have been *in* Little Village."

"But what about the kids?" you cry out, and "Come on! Don't do this. Not on their first day of school." But Aristeo is adamant: "I'm not going to support the school if it's not in Little Village. Good luck." And he hangs up.

You call Elias, but he's reading from the same script. "What should I tell the families?" you ask. He says something ridiculous like, "Move the school back, then I can support you, but where it is now, I can't."

"What do I tell the kids?

"Tell them *you* moved the school."

Jilted, you announce to the kids, the parents, the reporter, the teachers, board members, and your mom that Artiseo and Elias will not be speaking today.

Without a political base, you and the school are out there alone with a slumlord heading the board. You recruit other board members. You even get a VP as treasurer who is from one of the most powerful and far-reaching banks in the nation.

In September, you write a CPS charter application in order to secure the school's longevity and independence from Infinity. Simultaneously, you run a school on the fumes of less than $5,373 per student, serve as part-time security guard, part-time receptionist, and you bring in snacks for students daily because for some reason CPS just will not fulfill the school's right to breakfast and lunch. You call CPS food services three times a day begging for food, to no avail. You spend a lot of your own money feeding kids who don't need to starve during the day when so many of them starve at night.

If you do start a school, always try to remember the reasons why you wanted to start a school in the first place.

One day, one of the three teachers for your 45 students gets laryngitis after teaching like there's no tomorrow in this place with no breakfast, no lunch, no political base or support, no extra funding, no real administration beyond you, and 13-year-old Latino Two-Six and African American Gangster Disciple gang recruits trying to earn their stripes while in school. So you're teaching teachers how to teach students how to resolve conflicts, dismantle notions of difference, construct projects with the kids that will help them begin to see how they've been set up to ignore each other's humanity and common contexts. Teachers teach equity, give the students a voice they've never had, and the kids become righteous about things like black and Latino rights to a mutual sort of peace and justice.

You design City as a small school. Its program draws on already existing models like the Met in Rhode Island, the Urban School of San Francisco, Hampshire College in Massachusetts, and Colorado College in Colorado Springs. You have intentionally designed a school where all staff are allied with City's stated aim of college preparation and admission for all students. Soon you will propose to the charter board review committee that it is this overarching objective that will enable the school to practice and use learning and teaching methodologies that not only scaffold toward, but also actually model a liberal arts college curriculum. The school will be and is already based in habits of learning and instructional practices that produce academic inquiry and engagement, critical thinking, a sound sense of the past, a scientific frame of mind, quantitative reasoning abilities, and the ability to deal with large quantities of knowledge. And this all within the context of an extreme shortfall of resources.

When you finally present your charter application to the Chicago Public Schools charter review board, you tell them that a City education is a partnership between student, school, and family. Using anecdotes, you demonstrate to them that the school's small class size and school community allow faculty to develop an individual learning plan for each student that is based on their academic and social interests. Small groups, or advisories, of 15 students work with one teacher all 4 years of high school. Distinguished from the traditional definition of *advisory*, students' time with their advisor at City serves three functions. Advisory is a permanent *group* of 15 students and one advisor. It's also a *place*, the actual classroom where students and advisor gather for teaching and learning. Teaching during advisory is a combination of independent academic work, direct instruction, and cooperative group work. Lastly, advisory is a *time* when students and advisor meet every Monday, Wednesday, and Friday.

You have created a school where, together, teacher and student decide on a course of study, an independent learning plan that can include college classes, and independent academic projects that fulfill City's graduation requirements. Twice weekly, students participate in real work in internships connected to their interests and passions that are located throughout the city of Chicago.

The charter proposal requires details about assessment because, of course, Chicago is concerned about testing, and the 3-year-old NCLB act that has as its core standardized testing. But City won't concede to testing, and as a charter, it won't have to. You explain that City students are assessed based on quarterly demonstrations of work and academic portfolios, called Exhibitions. All learning is geared toward what a student wants to know and needs to learn in order to fulfill their personal goals and dreams. City teachers (called advisors) possess a strong interest in student-centered learning and they are committed to collaborative work with students, families, school staff, and you, the director.

Learning at City is not constrained by the school day or the school year. In response to adolescent brain research, City's school day begins at 10:00 a.m. Students are encouraged to pursue their interests and grow academically, and are given credit for activities outside of the school day and the school year. Every student's work is documented on an Independent Learning Plan, created and updated each quarter with the Learning Team comprised of the student, parents, advisor, and mentor as well as the Learning Specialist if a student has an Individual Education Plan (IEP). The curriculum, learning environment, use of time during the school day, choice of workshops or college classes, focus and depth of investigation in City's five areas of study are all based on a student's individual interests, talents, and needs; and students with IEPs follow the same process, also personalized to their needs.

City's five areas of study are housed within five academic schools, which provide a framework for the course of study. The five schools house the subject disciplines and provide a framework for study and the discipline objectives around which the student and advisor organize the Independent Learning Plan. The School of Aesthetics focuses on art-making. The School of Cultural and Global Studies emphasizes the critical examination of issues related to society, culture, social institution, and social change. The School of Humanities focuses on broadening the depth of a student's development and understanding of text, genre, analytical prose, and performance writing as ways to deepen an understanding of self, other, and difference as well as literate communication across the genres. The School of Mathematical Sciences provides the education and experience necessary to learn applied, problem-based mathematics, preparing students for the use of mathematics in real-world situations. The School of Natural Science is where students develop a scientific frame of mind and a way to apply a set of theories, methods, and data for understanding the world.

The Schools provide a process and way of thinking in a particular discipline, i.e., students learn to think scientifically; become quantitative reasoners; develop their own artistic ideas; develop a sense of the past; use a target language to communicate within and beyond the classroom setting; and read and write critically, creatively, and analytically. In the process, they become bi- or multi-lingual writers, artists, historians, critical theorists, and transdisciplinarians. As City grows, the plan is to hire strategically so that by 2005–2006, it has an advisor who is an expert in each of the disciplines represented by the five schools. One of City's guiding principles is to do what is best for the kids, appropriately challenging and supporting at the right time, not dictating or punishing, but problem-solving and mediating. The advisor's job is to promote growth by knowing each of their 15 students well. Students are responsible for following their interests and passions in the city and in their project work. They are also responsible for contributing and participating positively and productively to the city and the school community.

After you present your charter application, one of the charter review committee members says to the nods of others in the room, City is "the way all Chicago schools should be."

Don't believe the hype. And certainly don't keep a school going on hype alone.

With greater financial support, your school certainly has the potential to be exceptionally vibrant. The school has vision, a love of learning and teaching, strong academics and arts, a commitment to adolescent life, a dedication to building community and using the city as classroom, and despite the troubles that come, students from the opposing and segregated West and South sides of Chicago make their own rules like "No Gang Banging at the Crib," which means no gang activity in their home, which they very much consider City as Classroom School to be.

Once dumped by Aristeo and Elias, gracious educators at Small Schools Workshop like Susan and Mike Klonsky and John Ayers from Leadership for Quality Education all do their best to cast a net of support around you. But there is no one who steps in to guide you through Chicago's complex and political education network like Aristeo and Elias. You are afloat on a drifter with holes that no number of educators can pull back to the political center of education in Chicago. Of course, the problems are not all the fault of the broken relationship with Elias and Aristeo, and today you understand and know better.

Realize that your start-up is a set-up, a purposeful scheme to punish not you or the kids directly, but maybe just to punish, for reasons unknown, the men who negotiate hard for your school, or maybe just to push you out in order to give your facility to a different school with more political and economic backing. Who knows?

What you do know is that Chicago Public Schools' food services has neither given you a refrigerator, a cafeteria worker, nor breakfast and lunch for your kids each and every morning for 3 months. You just don't know, and probably never will, what compels them to ignore the voice mails that you leave every day asking "Where's the morning milk?" and "Where's our kids' lunch?"

One day, there's a surprise visit from a CPS official who's "checking in." This is just a couple of days after your two worst teachers quit because neither thought going on a week-long honeymoon during school or teaching kids by threatening or screaming at them was such a big deal. Is it just bad luck that every CPS sub is booked and because of NCLB you can't find a "qualified" teacher to take their place?

You now have one teacher for all 45 kids. You shuffle the CPS inspector from your office to the classroom of the one teacher left. You tell your first political fib when she asks, "Where are the other teachers?" You squeak out, "On a field trip."

"Where's your cafeteria?" she asks. You explain that the building has a cafeteria downstairs, but until you grow, the kids eat in their classrooms. The inspector says, "No, I mean where's the food and where's the cook?" You unload and tell her about all the calls and how hard it was to open City, but you don't dare tell her that you only have one teacher. The inspector calls you the poster child for principal endurance.

The next day, the school's door buzzer rings and there stands a woman dressed in cafeteria white. Next comes a refrigerator, then comes milk, then come boxes with CPS's nasty-but-oh-so-welcome packaged victuals. We get plasticized hot dogs, PB&J, once-grilled cheese, and very happy kids.

Don't start a school using a model that only includes three teachers if two of those teachers have never taught before and one just graduated from teacher ed. And realize there is trouble with a teacher's integrity when during the second week of school you're wondering, Where in the world is teacher So-and-So? and your students, noticing everything, figure out how unenlightened you are and notify you that teacher So-and-So is on his honeymoon.

After a week of you and your remaining teacher going it alone in the classroom with 45 kids, you look in the mirror and notice that you're looking presidential. In just a short time, gray hairs are popping up in bunches. And your sole teacher? She's got laryngitis. The doctor tells her "If you talk, you'll really lose your voice. So not one word." For 2 weeks, you end up teaching everything, running the administrative office, managing the books, sometimes even guarding the door, and plunging daily the toilets in the basement. Two board members who are like Isis and Superman keep the school supplied with toilet paper and the sanitary pads the girls can't afford to buy at home. Other board members donate books. And you, you give the school everything until your credit card statement balance reads close to $10,000.

One morning at 6:30 a.m., you call your godmother and just cry, shake from fear, scream real loud just once, because for 2 weeks you've run the school alone. Then you hear the kids come in and somehow you re-absorb all of it, act like all of this is normal, and carry on.

*   *   *   *   *   *

On December 14, 2004, the *Chicago Tribune* reports, "Proposals for five new charter schools are poised to be approved at the January Chicago Board of Education meeting." City as Classroom School is one of them. You get a phone call from a member of the charter review committee, who is already helping you make plans for your bilingual students, and fellow educators are spreading rumors that City's got a charter.

Winter break arrives. With charter rumors in the air, you decide to begin to move at least partially into the full model of City as best you can on what little money City is using to breathe. You hire math, Spanish, and history teachers and one new advisor, solidify the CPS special education resource person, get the classrooms and halls painted, install a makeshift computer lab, and make the security guard full-time. The kids come back and for the first time the school begins to soar.

But something must have happened between December 14 and January 14.

Somebody's mind got changed. Some Chicago dynamic of power got played. You are told by a reputable source, "Somebody struck a deal. Somebody shook somebody's hand."

On the dead media weekend, just before 3:00 p.m. on the Friday before the Martin Luther King Jr. holiday, CPS calls: "I'm sorry, you didn't get a charter. But we expect you to stay open."

They say the school should stick around, grow, and strengthen.

"On what?" you ask. "Air?"

Not only have you lost the charter, but you're also forced to act like you didn't want it in the first place by submitting a letter of withdrawal to CPS, which they request to be delivered as soon as possible. They say without it City will never again be able to submit a charter application.

Right now, the school is barely surviving on its $290,000 budget. Your contract with the local charter school ends in August, and that means City will have no status—not as a charter, not as a public school. On top of this, CPS and the local charter school aren't getting along and Nettie keeps intimating that they want to shut Infinity down. You know that without the $250,000 from the federal charter schools grant and other financing, the school can't maintain itself, and the kids will suffer. And you know, of course, CPS knows this is the case, too.

You make a plan with City's board.

Even though the teachers are sorry to lose their jobs and lose the idea that is City, they know that without money, the school can't survive. So, together, you shut the school down mid-year. You use every education connection you've established in your 3 plus years in Chicago, and you move every kid out of City within 2 weeks to schools that are right for each of the kids. You get them into schools where they'll be safe. You know this is the right thing to do. Summer is a dangerous time for these kids. You don't want them lingering for a semester in City's arms all sad and hopeless, and then spend a summer contemplating dropping out because they have no school. Moving the kids out now allows them to acclimate to a new school during the second semester while the academic year is still in session.

The situational and somewhat political acuity with which you shut down City—how you beg, push, and ensure that your kids get into good schools—makes you realize that Chicago has taught you a few things after all. It took you a minute, but you are finally seeing that power is in the geography of education, and power is all about politics in Chicago.

If you want to start a school in a major city in the United States, you'll need to understand from roots to stem the city's particular politics surrounding its geography, because it's these very politics that could determine whether your school opens (and closes). One of the many bottom lines in this school start-up business is this: Don't start a school 3 years after Senator Ted Kennedy co-authors a bill for standards-based education reform and 2 years after it is signed into law by George W. Bush, because this law, the Elementary and Secondary Education Act, or NCLB, *will make markets out of school districts, and buyers out of corporations, real estate developers and parents already desperate to escape under-resourced and neglected schools.*

If you plan to start a school, conduct research on the city in which you plan to open. If you find that it has something called a Commercial Club, don't be naïve and think that starting a school in a city that has a Commercial Club just means you're starting a school in a city that has a Commercial Club, especially when that city is Chicago—a city governed by quid pro quo deals utilizing Capone-style methods, a city where word has it that former mayor Richard M. Daley, once the longest-running mayor, signals his approval of your good intentions not with a handshake or a nod, not with a pat on the back, but with you and he in his office and the lighting of a stogie, and that's whether you smoke or not.

What does it matter, you say, if this club of mostly white men is "comprised of senior business, professional, educational and cultural leaders who seek to address social and economic issues of importance to the Chicago region" (CCC, n.d., online)? What does it matter if its membership reads like a Who's Who of the Fortune Global 500s and includes people like Edward M. Liddy, chairman, president, and CEO of Allstate, which in 2005 makes over $1.765 billion in profits (Allstate Corporation, 2006; or Thomas J. Pritzker, chair of Global Hyatt, who acquires the $300 million-a-year AmeriSuites chain (Bloomberg, 2004); or the governor of Illinois, and presidents of the private schools Northwestern University and University of Chicago? And what if that roster of financial kings and some queens, notably, does not include the state's public university, University of Illinois?

You still might think that none of this really matters to the start-up of your school and its ability to win a charter, because during all your feasibility studies for the school, if you did any, you probably never thought to conduct something like a corporate dominion study. What's that? you ask. What does it matter if the Commercial Club was "founded in 1877 by a group of 17 businessmen who believed Chicago needed a strong and cohesive civic force" (CCC)? In fact, you might think, sounds pretty noble.

What if you find out that this group of 17 white businessmen and their progeny believed this civic force could "shape the course of the city's development" (CCC), indeed, shape the course of its educational system? Might you then understand that it actually does matter that starting a school in a city like Chicago 2 years after NCLB has transformed school districts into markets; corporations into public contractors; local federal

*housing authorities accessories to the dismantling of public housing
and promotion of private real estate development; public housing into
$350,000 condos; and public schools into charters, which have the
Commerical Club's Civic Committee as trustees who allow Allstate, for
example, to partner with a Chicago-based corporation like American
Quality Schools, the Westside Ministers Coalition, and the Austin African-
American Business Networking Association in order to open Austin
Business and Entrepreneurship Academy (Dean, 2006)? Perhaps then will
you see the connections, and the coalitions between land, schools and
money, and why they matter?*

*Of course, if you do plan to start a school in a city like Chicago where
the Commercial Club has a Civic Committee, where the Civic Committee
has an education initiative, and where the Education Committee of the
Civic Committee of the Commercial Club has been involved in Chicago
school reform "as well as the establishment of charter schools" (CCC) for
the last 20 years, you can venture a pretty good guess that some of the
club's members will certainly see public schools as private commodities
like those they buy and sell during their day jobs at Abbott Laboratories,
Allstate Corporation, American Airlines, Ernst & Young, Exelon, Federal
Reserve Bank of Chicago, Kraft Foods, Hyatt Hotels, McDonald's,
Motorola, PricewaterhouseCoopers, Sara Lee Corporation, United
Continental Holdings, Walgreens, and about 486 other national and
multinational corporations.*

In the end, the dream of a new school and the heartfelt-risk-everything
commitment to the kids—the belief or fact that a particular type of process-
based learning; a certain type of meaningful, differentiated instruction; the
relevance of an active critical pedagogy in the lives of the kids and their families—does not matter. Not enough. Because these things can't be bought or
sold, traded, or used in the education market. Educational ideals like yours
create interchange instead of exchange, and the kind of social exchange they
make, the kind of futures they produce, the kind of benefit to a school that
they construct loses out to the business relationships required today to start
up and sustain a school.

The problem for you is that before you opened your school, you didn't understand that starting a school is not just about ideas, innovation, and imagination; it's not just about doing the right thing. Educational vision isn't like
business vision; it isn't a substance that can produce the kind of economic and
political relationships people need to get a school started and keep it open.

In August 2004, you start a school in Chicago. In February 2005,
you shut it down. So when you tell the story about starting up City as
Classroom School in Chicago, two years after NCLB makes markets out

of school districts—and buyers out of corporations, real estate developers, and parents already desperate to escape under-resourced and neglected schools—don't forget to tell people how much you didn't understand about the contemporary education economy or what former mayor Daley calls the "business of education."[8] Tell them about how much schooling for the public now pivots on the very conception that public education's primary concern is that of financial transactions, the art and science of politics, political attitudes and positions, the aggregate and complex of relationships of power and authority. In other words, the business of education is really about the politics of education, the geography of education, the economics of education, and hardly about the art of teaching and learning.

If you do start a school, and if you do have to shut down your school, make sure the last thing that you do is guarantee that all the bills are paid before you return the key.

Finally, make sure the last installment of tuition that includes Title I and/or Temporary Assistance for Needy Families funds from the state goes right into the hands of the phone company and utility company and accountant and every other business with which you contracted. Because $35,000 is more than enough to pay off all the school's debts. Don't turn the school's bank account over to your board chair. Don't let the chair and the treasurer assure you that they'll "take care of everything."

Be prepared.

Things like that $10,000 donation your board chair made early on might just turn into an expense and get reimbursed. And months, and even several years after you close the school, Chicago's utility providers will come knocking on your door—even if you move 400 miles away—expecting you, the unemployed former principal of the school, to pay up.

Well, hindsight is 20/20, right? It's only now that you're cognizant of how politically immature you were, how hopeful and stubborn you were when City was a possibility. Head down, you plowed through the start-up of that school, ignoring all the obvious alerts and conspicuous obstacles. It had something to do with your commitment to Las Madres; it had a lot to do with kids and who City kids were, who they had become by the time the school closed, and who they could have become had the school gained a charter. It also had to do with who you were then, a person you barely recognize now. You just didn't believe in "No" or "Stop" when it came to building something good for kids. And if I may be blunt, I think you were also kind of stupid, just plain ig'nant, as they used to say in the neighborhood in which you grew up.

Schooling is political, says your mama, just like everything else in this country, but it can feel personal, can't it, baby?

This was City's mission: Representing the knowledge, ability, and imagination of urban youth, City as Classroom School's mission is to build generations of public intellectuals motivated by their own interests and creativity, using the city of Chicago as their classroom. And for a little while, the kids, their families, the teachers, and I, we almost lived it.

NOTES

1. From a note to Constance Webb, which C.L.R. James included on the back of his essay, "Dialectical Materialism and the Fate of Humanity" (James, 1996).

2. This passage represents a collage of text from an article by education scholar David Stovall (2005) and student statistics from the "Illinois Interactive Report Card." In 2011, the percentages of poor students between the schools remain dramatically disparate. Ninety-seven percent of Farragut students are poor compared with Northside's 35% and Payton's 33%. Enrollment and graduation rates remain just as widely divergent. Farragut has 697 more students than Northside College Prep, and 863 more than Payton. Fifty-two percent of Farragut's students graduated in 2010, compared with 100% of Northside and 99% of Payton students.

3. The enormity of displacement is certainly transformative. The Plan for Transformation is the "largest redevelopment effort of public housing in the history of the nation" (CHA, 2009). Approved by the federal Department of Housing and Urban Development, "by the end of the Plan, 25,000 units of housing will be renovated or built new . . . transforming the culture and structure of public housing" (CHA, n.d., online).

4. All names have been changed.

5. In 1996, Illinois passed a law allowing charter schools to be created. One of the main aspects of the law included a provision that stated: "The number of charter schools that can be created is limited to 75 in Chicago (five of which are dedicated to drop out recovery schools) and 45 outside of Chicago" (INCS, n.d., online).

6. If you had read page 4 of the December 2000 Federal Reserve Bank of Chicago's report, "The Homeownership and Financing Experience in Two Chicago Minority Neighborhoods," you might have known these little facts: "While the total housing units in Little Village have remained virtually unchanged from its 1960 level, the population has increased by 33 percent. The vacancy rate has declined from 44 percent in 1960 to 7 percent in 1990. To a major extent, new housing construction projects have been difficult to undertake because of *limited geographical space available*" (Rhine, p. 4). Emphasis here is certainly yours, in hindsight. Of course, you just moved to Chicago 2 years ago, and you never even knew, let alone considered, doing this kind of homework in neighborhood economics and property financing before starting up a school. But that's exactly why you had no business ever starting a school.

7. Part of City's philosophy was to educate the whole child and to make them aware of their hearts, minds, and bodies. The students' addiction to the MSG in hot chips sold by companies like Lays inspired a City history/theater teacher to

write a performance poem called "What Is They Feedin Our Kids," which he later performed on Russell Simmon's *HBO Def Poetry Jam* in 2007. See Idris Goodwin perform "What Is They Feedin Our Kids" at http://www.youtube.cf/watch?v=ppCRG2y3YGM.

8. This quotation is taken from a Chicago Public Schools announcement of the Renaissance 2010 education initiative on June 24, 2004. "Ren '10," as it is known by Chicago educators, proposed to shut down 60 schools and open 100 new ones. In fact, CPS opened 103 schools by 2010 (Chicago Public Schools, n.d., online). Quotations from the announcement were once accessible online (but no longer are) at *School Planning & Management* <http://www.peterli.com/archive/spm/711.shtm>.

REFERENCES

Ahmed, A., & Little, D. (2008, December 26). Chicago, america's most segregated big city. *Chicago Tribune*. Retrieved from http://articles.chicagotribune.com/2008-12-26/news/0812250194_1_racial-steering-douglas-massey-neighborhoods

Allstate Corporation. (2006, March 27). Notice of 2006 annual meeting, proxy statement, 2005 annual report. Northbrook, IL: Allstate Corporation.

Bloomberg Businessweek. (2004, December 9). Hyatt: Quite a housecleaning. Retrieved from http://www.businessweek.com/bwdaily/dnflash/dec2004/nf2004129_0663_db016.htm

Chicago Housing Authority (CHA). (2009). The plan at 10. Retrieved from http://www.thecha.org/pages/the_plan_at_10/49.php

Chicago Housing Authority (CHA). (n.d.). The plan for transformation. Retrieved from http://www.thecha.org/pages/the_plan_for_transformation/22.php

Chicago Public Schools (CPS). (n.d.). Who we are. Retrieved from http://cps.edu/NewSchools/Pages/WhoWeAre.aspx

Commercial Club of Chicago (CCC). (n.d.). Retrieved from http://www.commercialclubchicago.org/

Dean, T. (2006, August 30). Austin business academy opens: First of three renaissance 2010 "small" schools in one building. *Austin Weekly News*.

Federal Reserve Bank of Chicago. (2000, December). The homeownership and financing experience in two chicago minority neighborhoods. Chicago: Sherrie Rhine and Maude Toussaint-Comeau.

Illinois Network of Charter Schools (INCS). (n.d.). Charter school law. Retrieved from http://incschools.org/charters/why_charter_schools/charter_school_law/

James, C. L. R. (1996). *Special delivery: The letters of C. L. R. James to Constance Webb, 1939–1948*. (A. Grimshaw, Ed. and Intro.) Cambridge, MA: Blackwell.

Stovall, D. (2005, May). From hunger strike to high school: Youth development, social justice and school formation. *Great Cities Institute Working Paper* (GCP-05-01).

8

Khalil Gibran International Academy

From Dream to Nightmare

DEBBIE ALMONTASER

> The New York City Department of Education succumbed to the very bias that the creation of the school was intended to dispel and a small segment of the public succeeded in imposing its prejudices on D.O.E. as an employer.
> —*Debbie Almontaser v. NYCDOE*, 2010

We all have dreams. On our optimistic days, we hope they will miraculously come true. As an educator, I dreamed of one day leading a school. I ended up with more than just leading one. In 2006, I led the creation of the first Arabic dual-language public school in the United States, the Khalil Gibran International Academy. That dream, more beautiful than I could have imagined, soon became a nightmare. This is my story of the rise and fall of an idea that was too potent for our time.

THE DREAM

In a climate of great post 9/11 misunderstanding and mistrust, one of my objectives was to educate the broader New York City public about their Arab American neighbors. In 2005, I was immersed in working with the mayor's office in the inauguration of Arab Heritage Week. In the midst of this, New Visions for Public Schools, a school reform organization, decided to act on the development of an Arabic/Hebrew language high school with a co-existence theme. The man behind the idea at New Visions was Adam Rubin, a Jewish American who longed for a school that would be a model for Arab and Jewish coexistence. After 6 months of searching for an Arab American educator to work on the development of such a school, Adam contacted me at the recommendation of the New York City Department of Education (DOE), the mayor's Office of Immigrant Affairs, and an Arab American woman at a falafel stand in Brooklyn. Yes, at a falafel stand. This confirmed for Adam how well known I was as an educator and community organizer.

Weeks later, I met with Adam. We spent close to 2 hours speaking about such a school. His last words to me that day as he walked me to the elevator were, "This is an opportunity for you to merge the two things you love most: education and bridge building between east and west. The time has come for you to fulfill that destiny." A couple of weeks later, I met with the president of New Visions, school designers, and Adam. I left this meeting ready to spearhead the school's development. I put my faith in New Visions, based on its long history of establishing dozens of new schools in New York City. I felt that I was finally going to be able to fulfill my long overdue dream of becoming a school leader—starting a new dual-language English-Arabic school where students could become experts on that part of the world.

In the next several days, questions raced through my mind: Could such a school get approved? Is New York City, 6 years after 9/11, ready for such a school? Will there be interest in the school within the Arab community and the broader New York City community? Will New Yorkers support the development? I knew back then that some people would view such a project in a negative light, especially in the years after 9/11. I knew that the only way to get a school like this approved was to show there was a dire need and that a variety of community groups were prepared to support it.

In the months ahead, I began to learn about the process of establishing a school from scratch by attending DOE new school forums and the New Visions school creation sessions. New Visions and I also learned from linguists that teaching both Arabic and Hebrew was impossible on a secondary level. Their recommendation was just to teach Arabic, especially since there was funding to teach this language.

Simultaneously, I began an informal feasibility study with educators, academics, community and civic leaders, politicians, community-based organization leaders within the Arab American community, and others, including clergy of different faiths, parents, and students, as well as 9/11 families. I wanted to learn their reactions to establishing a new dual-language English-Arabic school, the need for a school to teach Arabic/cultural studies, and whether the timing was right, but most important, I wanted to get their support. Every individual I spoke with saw the potential for this school to become a place of learning and healing, and they offered their support.

To start a New Visions school, we needed a lead partner agency to be the fiscal conduit for the $400,000 Gates Foundation Grant. New Visions recommended a couple of higher education institutions and a couple of well-established non-profit groups as possible partners. We explored other possibilities, including the Middle East Department at the City College of New York's Graduate Center, which declined to partner due to a shortage of staff and financial capacity. However, my heart was set on having an institution that was grounded in Arab culture and connected to the community for a sense of pride and community ownership.

In the aftermath of 9/11, Arabs, Muslims, and South Asians were traumatized by backlash and discrimination, as well as by government crackdowns under the Patriot Act that led to members of these communities being detained and deported. In these communities there was a great deal of mistrust and suspicion of programs initiated by local and federal government agencies—especially ones pertaining to the learning of Arabic. I wanted the Arab, Muslim, and South Asian communities to know that this school would not be a FBI or CIA front, but a public school for the community and for all New Yorkers, regardless of their ethnic, religious, or racial background. My choice to engage all of these stakeholders was essential to empower members of my community, get their blessings, and win long-lasting support for the school. As an educator and bridge builder among communities, I valued this process.

With my help, New Visions hosted a gathering for the Arab American leadership of New York to introduce the small school development process. It encouraged the community to compete with other groups seeking to open new schools. The result would be the first Arabic dual-language public school in New York City—joining 70 dual-language schools in various languages where students become proficient in both languages. Among those who attended the New Visions gathering were leaders whom I consulted during the informal feasibility study. By the end of the New Visions presentation, many Arab American leaders had been sold on the concept of the school and they wanted to strategize next steps.

Following the meeting at New Visions, the Arab American community members who had attended elected me to chair the meetings, since I was most familiar with the new small school process and had a relationship with New Visions. I accepted the role and facilitated the learning process to establish the school with New Visions and the DOE. The committee was charged with identifying the lead agency and identifying a highly qualified educator to lead the school. Even though I wanted to lead the school, I wanted the Arab American community to choose the school leader. My vision was about empowering the community and having them feel a sense of ownership in the school. To do this, I had to put my personal aspirations of developing and leading the school aside to enable the community to be fully involved in the process.

I informed New Visions about this process and asked them to honor it. This was the first time they had ever experienced such a process. In the usual New Visions process, a self-selected educator put a design team together, looked for a lead agency, and worked on developing a school. New Visions' biggest fear was that the community might choose someone who was not well known and connected in New York City for such a school to prosper. I reassured them that the community was going to choose the best person for the job, and I also promised New Visions that if I were not the final candidate, I would assist and fully support the community's choice.

After a 2-month process, which included an arduous question and answer session, the community vote determined that the Arab American Family Support Center best met the New Visions and DOE application criteria. They were well known as a social service agency with a focus on youth development and had diversified funding and a track record of raising foundation funds.

Once the lead agency process was complete, a principal selection committee was formed, consisting of a few community organization heads and academics, which put out the call for the principal position. Three weeks later, they called for an interview with a very qualified Arab American gentleman and me. I left the interview confident, but couldn't stop thinking about how I might not be chosen, how I would personally deal with this decision, and whether I would be able to work with the final candidate. The next day, I received a call from the selection committee congratulating me on being the finalist for the position based on my articulation of an inclusive and innovative vision.

The community also had to decide where the school should open upon approval. We all felt that New York City is a microcosm of the world. And, Brooklyn, as one of the most diverse boroughs in the nation and home to one of the oldest Arab communities in America, was the perfect site for Khalil Gibran International Academy (KGIA). We included in the proposal that the school should be in Brooklyn and lobbied for this location once the school was approved.

THE WORK OF THE DESIGN TEAM

As the project director and principal, I was charged with the next phase of project development. I canvassed the city for individuals I knew would want to be a part of the development in order to get a design team together to design and write the proposal for the school to be approved by New Visions and DOE. Every person I approached didn't have to think twice about being a part of the design team, which was comprised of educators, former principals, assistant principals, prospective parents, community members, professionals, and students who reflected the great ethnic and religious diversity of New York City. There were members of the team who spoke Arabic, Hebrew, Spanish, French, and Chinese. We even had a government employee, Brooklyn Borough President Marty Markowitz, who was fully supportive and assigned his education advisor to serve on the design team.

Simultaneously, the need for community partners to support the school was essential. Organizations both in the Arab American and the larger community gave the design team endorsement letters to accompany the proposal. Incredibly, we had more than 11 partnering groups offering internships in law and medicine, conflict resolution and cultural diversity training, and cultural arts education. Partnering organizations included the Tanenbaum Center for Inter-religious Understanding, the Brooklyn Museum, Morningside Center for Social Responsibility, Brooklyn Conservatory for Music, Columbia University's Teachers College, Lutheran Hospital, the Alwan for the Arts center, and several others.

Starting in July 2006, the design team and I, along with the Arab American Family Support Center, worked for the next 6 months to meet the New Visions and DOE proposal deadlines. The first step was getting the executive summary approved, so that we would have the opportunity to submit an entire proposal. We were competing with 40 teams seeking New Visions' partnership and more than 200 teams across the city. In the end, we were one of four teams to be selected by New Visions and one of 80 that the DOE approved to submit a complete new school proposal.

Our goal was to create a school that emphasized inquiry-based, project-based learning that exposed students to multiple perspectives. This approach was designed to foster the critical thinking, problem-solving, and communication skills necessary for our students to become ambassadors of peace and hope, young people who would be able to create bridges of understanding across cultural and other differences.

With Arabic language skills increasingly in demand, the Arabic language program was a critical component of the curriculum. Students were going to develop the ability to understand the thoughts, beliefs, and ideas of the Arab peoples, positioning them to become cross-cultural ambassadors, and preparing them to pursue international careers. The curriculum was going to provide students exposure to a wide variety of cultures and perspectives while having a primary focus on learning about the richness and diversity of Arab culture and history.

As stated in our proposal, "The very existence of this school is to provide the needed mechanism for a diverse population of students to learn the Arabic language, the culture and its contributions." KGIA was intended to graduate "students with a deep understanding of Arabic culture and different cultural perspectives; a love of learning; and a desire for excellence with integrity" in order to prepare them for "leadership in today's constantly changing global world." Although I worried that the DOE would fear approving an Arabic dual-language school in the aftermath of 9/11, one week after submitting our final proposal I received an email from the DOE stating that we had been granted an interview date to make our case on why KGIA should be approved. Our 13-member design team spoke confidently and passionately in front of a 10-person panel comprised of educators, school superintendents, central DOE employees, and school reform organization heads. It was one of the most grueling moments and at the same time the most gratifying moment of my life. We clearly described our mission and vision, and we answered every question coherently with no hesitation. I had no doubt that we were going to be approved.

However, in January 2007, when the first batch of new schools was approved and announced, KGIA was not among them. But, on Monday, January 29, the call we had been waiting for finally came, verbally approving KGIA. The DOE saw the need for such a school among the many other small new schools approved. On February 11, 2007, the DOE issued a press statement naming KGIA among 40 other schools being approved for the 2007–2008 school year. I was finally able to breathe easy and prepare for the next stage of the process.

KGIA made its national debut on February 12, 2007, in *The New York Times* (Gootman, 2007), as one of 40 other schools to be approved. In the days after, Internet bloggers began to attack the school, but although we were aware of this hysteria, we remained focused on the work ahead.

PREPARING TO OPEN KGIA

Although KGIA was approved to open at the beginning of the 2007–2008 school year, a school site was not listed on the press release. As the principal, I was privy to location possibilities. I refused to accept a couple of locations proposed by the DOE due to their remoteness from the communities the school was especially seeking to serve.

The final location determined was P.S. 282 in Park Slope, Brooklyn. The DOE notified the school administration that it was seeking to place KGIA there due to the amount of unused space in the building. In finding space for KGIA and other new schools across the five boroughs, the DOE made no attempt to engage the community in assessing whether its space plan was feasible. The DOE simply made school placement decisions on its own without any community engagement, leading many existing school communities to revolt against incoming new schools.

The protests of P.S. 282 parents sadly played out with KGIA landing on the front page of local papers. These papers fanned the flames with headlines like "Holy War! Slope Parents Protest Arabic School Plan" (Rubinstein, 2007) and "A Madrassa Grows in Brooklyn" (Pipes, 2007a), and "Arabic School Idea Is a Monstrosity" (Colon, 2007). After weeks of parent protests, the DOE abandoned its plan for P.S. 282 and shifted its focus to the Sarah J. Hale Campus in Boerum Hill, Brooklyn, where two schools were already sharing the building. Although KGIA again faced parental opposition, mostly from Middle School 447, the mayor's office cut deals to get KGIA placed on this campus.

Finally, KGIA had a home in a fourth-floor wing that was separate from the other two schools. KGIA was allocated three classrooms and two offices, enough for 60 students to begin as the inaugural class. Within weeks, the middle school parents had forced a change in these arrangements and KGIA was then moved to one of the most uninviting and isolated locations in the building: the first floor, consisting of an area where a run-down library had once existed, and a large cafeteria space directly outside the library area. The space was certainly not conducive to learning, but it was already July and student enrollment was under way. The DOE decided to partition the cafeteria space to make three classrooms and a main office with portable partitions. To make it up to the staff and me, the DOE's Office of New Schools promised us Smart Boards for each room and a class set of portable laptops, but they were never given to the school.

While all of this was happening, I was in the midst of the school start-up: creating job descriptions, school budgeting, ordering furniture and textbooks, DOE core curricula, interviewing potential staff, recruiting students, engaging the community, and dealing with media requests. I remained focused on the work at hand—not allowing the negative press and bigoted attacks to deter me. I constantly reminded myself that what I had ventured into was uncomfortable for people with narrow worldviews whose fears and misconceptions of anything Arab or Muslim stoked their actions.

Regardless, there was an incredible buzz of excitement about the school. Teachers from across the country were applying to teach at KGIA; they wanted to be a part of this historical institution. The staff hired was very diverse ethnically, culturally, and racially. Among the eight staff members, five languages were spoken: Arabic, French, Spanish, Greek, and Hebrew. The teachers were very excited to be part of the founding staff, despite the mounting opposition the school faced. They did not let the media frenzy deter their belief in the school or their confidence in my leadership.

In preparation for an anticipated journey, the staff engaged in 2 weeks of professional development where they became immersed in KGIA's mission and vision of developing global citizens who valued and celebrated diversity with the help of the Tanenbaum Center for Inter-religious Understanding. In addition, teachers began to develop their curriculum maps for the year in all subject areas and for the advisory program. They also began to prepare for the Summer Bridge Program that provides students and parents with an orientation to the school and helps to determine their children's academic standing for the coming school year. Shortly after, the two Arabic teachers went to Michigan State University for 2 weeks of training with other Arabic educators from across the country. The teachers learned how to teach Arabic and devise supplemental curricula to Scholastic's My Arabic Library curriculum.

During this time, we attended some middle school fairs to recruit students where KGIA's table had one of the longest lines for information. In addition, parents dropped in to our new site to learn about KGIA and what it had to offer. Families couldn't wait for the Summer Bridge program in August and the school year to begin. In total, by August 7, 2007, KGIA had 44 students who were officially registered and six others being processed.

AND THEN THERE WAS THE NIGHTMARE

While I was worried about when the furniture was going to arrive and the partitions would go up, those who sought to ensure that the school would never open tried everything in their power to undermine my efforts. When these groups saw that the DOE remained committed to opening the school, they shifted their attacks to me—the school's founding principal and director of the project. I was prepared for the attacks on the school, given its theme, but I didn't think that some of my fellow Americans would demonize me and try to make me into a caricature that was unrecognizable to me and the people who knew my work in New York City and knew me personally.

The people who attacked me were against my religion and my ethnicity; they were against Arabs and Muslims. They posted pictures of me in hijab (head scarf) on websites and blogs, and printed them in local papers along with false charges that I was a radical Islamist with an agenda to teach radicalism. They took my words in local and national papers out of context and distorted them. A 2007 *New York Sun* article, for example, cited a 2003 article about who was responsible for 9/11 and quoted me as saying, "I don't recognize the people who committed the attacks as either Arabs or Muslims" (Pipes, 2007b, online). They left out the second half of the quotation, which illustrated how I vehemently condemned those responsible for 9/11. It states, "Those people who did it have stolen my identity as an Arab and have stolen my religion" (Cohler-Esses, 2007, online).

I never thought I would be at the center of such attacks. Leading the charge with editorials in the *New York Sun* was Daniel Pipes, a so-called "expert" on the Middle East and head of the Middle East Forum, in addition to Jeffrey Wiesenfeld, a member of the Board of Trustees at City University of New York as well as a board member of the Jewish Community Relations Council. Along with Pamela Geller, from the Atlas Shrugs right-wing blog, and a few others, they started a group called "Stop the Madrassa Coalition." For the most part, the DOE countered some of the attacks by having the head of the Office of New Schools, Garth Harries, appear on *CNN* and *Fox*.

By July 2007, members of the Stop the Madrassa Coalition were appearing at events I attended and were verbally assaulting me with vicious anti-Arab and anti-Muslim rhetoric. The attacks were made up of vengeful rhetorical queries:

Will you be teaching children to hate Christians and Jews?
We heard that you don't believe 9/11 happened, and you deny it was Arabs/Muslims.
Why did you refuse to say whether or not Hamas and Hezbollah are terrorist organizations?
We have learned that you are a part of the U.S. history revisionist movement [which denies that the Holocaust occurred]?
Are you going to be teaching Sharia law?
Will you be segregating boys from the girls and holding prayers in school?

My attackers were all suggesting that, because the school's namesake, Khalil Gibran, was a Lebanese Christian (a renowned poet and philosopher of peace and understanding), and because I am an observant Muslim woman in hijab, I was unqualified to lead KGIA. What they neglected to see was a rigorously secular school required to meet the same curriculum and instructional standards as any New York public school. To stir up anti-Arab prejudice, the Stop the Madrassa Coalition constantly referred to me by my Arabic name, a name that I neither use professionally nor have used for many years. They even created and circulated a *YouTube* clip depicting me as an Islamic radical.

The attacks were driven by racism and bigotry based on growing anti-Arab, anti-Muslim sentiment in the country. In an interview with the *New York Sun*, a reporter asked me a question about Hezbollah and Hamas.

I asked her whether she would ask this of the 1,500 other public school principals. Her response was "No." The *Sun* viewed my response as a refusal and throughout the attacks on me, this sort of faulty and erroneous reporting continued. Opponents described the school that was being created to bridge the divides, dispel stereotypes, and prepare students to become global citizens ready to take on the challenges of the 21st century as a *Madrassa*, a word—literally meaning "school" in Arabic—now used to refer to schools in Pakistan known for indoctrinating children. Delays by KGIA's primary partners—New Visions and the Arab American Family Support Center—who were responsible for putting up a school website and hiring a communications person, meant that people did not have ready access to accurate information about the school. In the absence of a school website and a school marketing plan that would counter negative stories, the right wing controlled the narrative and the pressures continued to mount.

In August 2007, the Stop the Madrassa Coalition ignited a media firestorm that tenuously connected me to T-shirts made by a youth organization called Arab Women in the Arts and Media (AWAAM). The T-shirts said, "Intifada NYC." *New York Post* reporters aggressively sought my comments in response to the connection being made between the AWAAM T-shirts and me. Because the shirts had nothing to do with KGIA or with me, I saw no reason to discuss the issue with the media. At the DOE's insistence, a three-way phone interview with the reporter from the *New York Post*, a DOE press person, and me took place. During the interview, the reporter asked about my affiliation with AWAAM. I explained that there was no affiliation and explained that I was a member of the board of a social service organization that had permitted the group to run its summer youth program in the organization's office space.

The reporter then asked about the Arabic origin of the word *intifada*. I told him that the Arabic root word from which *intifada* originates means "shake off." I explained that the term has evolved over time and has different meanings for different people. I acknowledged that certainly for many, given the word's association with the Palestinian-Israeli conflict, a conflict in which thousands have died, the word is associated with violence. I reiterated that I would never affiliate myself with an individual or organization that would condone any violence. In response to a follow-up question, I expressed the belief that the teenage girls of AWAAM were not going to engage in a "Gaza-style uprising" in New York City, as the reporter had claimed. These were urban youth in a summer program that gave them the opportunity to engage in arts and media.

Sadly, the reporter from the *New York Post* distorted my words regarding the root word and made it seem like I minimized the historical context of the Intifada. The reporter wrote: "But Almontaser downplayed the significance of the T-shirts. 'The word [intifada] basically means 'shaking off.' That is the root word if you look it up in Arabic,'" she said (Bennett & Winter, 2007, online). Despite the fact that the article accurately reflected my view that I do not condone violence, the reporter intentionally neglected to report what I said regarding the fact *intifada* had evolved over time to mean uprising and had developed a negative connotation for many due to its connection to the Palestinian-Israeli conflict.

After the interview was published, friends and allies from the inter-faith community called to see what was going on. Those who knew how the *New York Post* operated paid the story no mind. However, others believed the story, regardless of my record and what they knew I stood for. The DOE press secretary called as well. He repeatedly asked why I had spoken about the T-shirts. My response was that I had not spoken about the T-shirts; I had, as an educator, discussed the root word of *intifada*, to give contextual information to a word about which many have limited knowledge. The press person who had been on the phone with me during the interview had no objection to what I said. She knew that I was doing my job as an educator. She did not interject or interrupt me as I talked to the *New York Post* reporter. In fact, after the interview, she called to inform me that I had done a good job.

A few hours after the interview, the DOE press secretary called again. After deliberation with the schools chancellor and senior leadership, he told me, the "best way" to deal with the mess created by the article was to issue a statement. I was delighted to do so. When we had spoken earlier that morning, I had emphasized to him the importance of demanding a retraction from the *New York Post*. To my dismay, however, the DOE had already crafted a very different statement—an apology:

> The use of the word "Intifada" is completely inappropriate as a
> t-shirt slogan. I regret suggesting otherwise. By minimizing the word's
> historical associations I implied that I condone violence and threats
> of violence. That view is anathema to me and the very opposite of my
> life's work. I have spent most of the last two decades working with
> religious and community leaders to build intergroup understanding
> and to promote non-violent solutions to conflict.

Knowing that I had neither said anything wrong nor offended anyone, making this statement was the last thing I wanted to do. Throughout the course of the interview, I had purposely focused on maintaining neutrality in order to avoid being plunged into the political arena. What I did was what authentic educators do: provide all perspectives on an issue and allow students to form their own conclusions.

Beginning that afternoon, the DOE and I began to work in parallel worlds with very little coordination or communication. After some back-and-forth about why an apology was not the appropriate approach, the press secretary maintained, "It is in your best interest to do as we advise if you want to see the school open." There was nothing I wanted more than to see this historic school open. I was deeply conflicted: The last thing that I wanted to do was to condemn AWAAM's right to freedom of expression, or the organization as a whole, which was providing a desperately needed service for young Arab women and girls of color.

I found myself being asked to speak against my own kind, which I would have had no problem doing if they were engaging in any illegal activity or if they were aiming to harm our country. I insisted on revising the statement with the understanding that the first sentence be nonnegotiable. I immediately worked on the statement and added the word *teenagers* to the first sentence and sent it back to the press secretary with a message requesting my approval before the final statement was sent out. I waited for hours, but heard nothing. I called and emailed the press office a few times, and then around 7:00 p.m., the DOE emailed me the final statement, which was an apology in my name that was no different from the statement that I had earlier rejected. At that point, I realized that my authority as principal was being completely ignored. To ensure that the school would open, I put my pride aside, compromised my views, and did not publicly protest their issuance of the apology, even though I knew full well that such a statement was going to exacerbate the situation.

As I had anticipated, things did get worse. The right-wing groups seized the moment to attack me for my follow-up response. The DOE changed course and decided I should have condemned the word intifada and not explained it. The department argued that I should have condemned the motives of the AWAAM.

By the end of the week, I was forced to resign by New Visions and Deputy Mayor Dennis Walcott, and all because I had done what any ethical educator would do: I seized the moment as a teachable one. Without taking any political position, I provided the root meaning of a word in response to a question and made it clear that the word has different meanings for different people. The people with whom I had worked closely and whom I trusted had, unconditionally and literally, reduced me to a word. And in so doing they had ignored my experience and qualifications.

August 9, 2007, marked a sad day for me. The DOE and New Visions forced me to abandon my American dream. Days after my forced resignation, the DOE and New Visions replaced me with Danielle Salzberg, a New Visions employee and former assistant principal who did not speak Arabic, had no cultural expertise, and no connection to New York City's Arab communities.

DOE officials should simply have said that it was clear that neither KGIA nor I had any connection to the T-shirts. They should have pointed out that I had devoted my entire adult life to the peaceful resolution of conflict and to building bridges between ethnic and religious communities. In other words, they should have said that the attacks upon me were utterly baseless.

From this incident, one can see how Arabic is being co-opted and manipulated by people who do not speak it. For example, Randi Weingarten, then president of New York City United Federation of Teachers (UFT) and now head of the American Federation of Teachers immediately attacked me in the *New York Post* without investigating what actually had happened. She argued that the word intifada should be condemned rather than defined. According to Weingarten, there was no place in education to discuss such a word, because to her it only connoted violence. Notions like this held and espoused by the teachers' union dealt a major blow to the educators whom Weingarten supposedly protected. What Weingarten and others who support censorship in education are doing to this day is endangering the integrity of the teaching profession.

In the weeks following my forced resignation from KGIA, I secluded myself to ensure that the school opened as promised. However, activists, educators, local and civic leaders, and New York City residents did not believe I simply resigned. They wanted answers from Mayor Bloomberg and the DOE. These individuals recognized that the supposed Middle East expert Daniel Pipes and other right-wing neo-conservative groups were launching a much wider campaign than that which had been set in motion against KGIA. Their objective was to cast doubt on and suspicion of Arab and Muslim U.S. citizens and community leaders with sterling credentials. In response to the attacks of conservative groups, activists, educators, and others decided to stand up for individuals such as me.

On August 20, 2007, concerned individuals organized a rally made up of people from different ethnic, racial, and religious communities in front of the DOE on Chambers Street in Manhattan. I was in disbelief that such a rally was going to take place, since I couldn't imagine myself at the center of a campaign demanding justice. I was always on the other end of campaigns—protesting injustice done to other people. In the sea of people, protesters held such signs as "Jewish UFTer for Debbie Almontaser" and "Bring Debbie Back!" I was deeply touched by the outpouring of support exhibited at the rally, which deepened my conviction to continue strengthening relations and building bridges of understanding among Christians, Muslims, and Jews, as well as other groups striving to create peaceful communities.

RECOVERING JUSTICE

Among the people who actively supported me was Alan Levine, a longtime civil rights attorney, a social justice activist as far back as the civil rights movement. Alan led the legal team for my case, arguing against my forced resignation. Our first point of action was getting my job back, by applying to the principalship posting for KGIA—a procedure every founding principal had to go through for appointment. Our second point of action was filing a claim in federal court against the DOE and New York City for infringing on my First Amendment rights in November 2007. The claim required a motion to the federal court for injunctive relief and it required the DOE to afford me a full and fair opportunity to be considered for the position of permanent principal of KGIA. In addition, we were arguing to have a disinterested person other than the chancellor finalize the appointment of the KGIA principal. The motion required an expedited trial, which was granted. After a 2-day trial in December 2007, Manhattan federal Judge Sidney Stein denied us the injunctive relief, and shortly after, we appealed.

At a Court of Appeals hearing in February 2008, the judges sharply criticized the city's handling of the controversy surrounding the school and me. One of the judges stated:

> I can't believe the city really wants to take that position, that if there
> is a disruptive response to a misleading article that unfairly quotes
> a city employee, then they get disciplined. That's a very unattractive
> position for a city to take (*Almontaser v. New York City Department
> of Education*, 2008).

Although it was refreshing to finally hear a judge state that I was unjustly treated, weeks later, the motion for injunctive relief was denied. However, the case was sent back to Judge Stein for reexamination of the First Amendment claim, which he had no interest in examining. In response, we appealed again and patiently waited for the oral argument date.

In the 10 days after my forced resignation, a variety of individuals and organization coalesced to form Communities in Support of KGIA (CIS-KGIA). This coalition was composed of more than 40 diverse groups, including AWAAM, Brooklyn for Peace, Center for Immigrant Families, Greater New York Labor-Religion Coalition, Jews for Racial and Economic Justice (JFREJ), and the Muslim Consultative Network. The groups' goals were to challenge what had happened to KGIA, support the vision of the school, speak out against the racism that had undermined it, and fight for a just and equitable public education system. CIS-KGIA worked closely with my legal team, which valued the importance of community organizing.

CIS-KGIA immediately developed a website (www.kgia.wordpress.com) to chronicle what was happening and what they as a coalition were doing to seek justice. This was one of the most interesting and inspiring campaigns in which one could ever wish to participate. CIS-KGIA was determined to hold the DOE and Randi Weingarten accountable for capitulating to a campaign fueled by Islamophobia and racism, and the group demanded my reinstatement. Their action plans included rallies; petitions; press conferences and media outreach; educational forums; and engagement with a broad array of civic and political leaders, community members, and academics. Simultaneously, CIS-KGIA was also organizing to ensure that KGIA was getting the support it needed to succeed.

CIS-KGIA was there at every turn of my case. In 2008, my lawyers also filed a discrimination complaint with the federal Equal Employment Opportunities Commission (EEOC). Its determination was released in March 2010 *(Debbie Almontaser v. NYC DOE)*, and offered me more relief and vindication than I could possibly have imagined. The EEOC ruling determined that my forced resignation was discriminatory on account of my "race, religion and national origin" and that the DOE had "succumbed to the very bias that creation of the school was intended to dispel." The EEOC declared that I "had no connection whatsoever" with the T-shirts and that "a small segment of the public succeeded in imposing its prejudices on the DOE as an employer."

The EEOC determination clearly demonstrated that they had performed a thorough investigation. However, Paul Marks, the city's deputy chief of labor and employment law in the Law Department of the DOE, was quoted in *The New York Times* claiming the DOE "in no way discriminated against Ms. Almontaser and she will not be reinstated." He went on to state "If she continues to pursue litigation, we will vigorously defend against her groundless allegations" (cited in Elliott, 2010, online).

KGIA TODAY

As months went by after the school's opening, teachers I had hired were disappointed by how the new administration compromised the school's mission and vision. The Arabic language program suffered immensely. Because the teachers I had hired chose to speak out, they were mistreated and finally driven out of the school by the third principal, Holly Anne Reichert, who replaced Ms. Salzberg. In its first couple of years, the school experienced a high rate of violent incidents and student suspensions, leading many families to pull their children out of the school.

For the second year of the school, in 2008–2009, the DOE decided to relocate KGIA to another school building, where it again faced some initial opposition from the parents whose children were already attending the school in which it would be housed. The new location was far from the Arab American community that KGIA had set out to serve. The school would be moved to P.S. 287 in the center of the largely African American Farragut projects, a difficult site to access by public transportation. KGIA staff and families did not learn of this move until they read about it in the newspaper. Once again, the DOE acted without parental and school-community input. In addition, prior to the move, the DOE had informed P.S. 287 families that KGIA would function as a middle school, rather than as the grade 6-12 school that KGIA planners had envisioned.

In March 2010, the school received its fourth principal after the EEOC determination had unearthed that there had been three Arab Americans who had applied for the position when I did, but the DOE selectively decided to pass them up. Shortly after the EEOC determination, the DOE abruptly removed Ms. Reichert and replaced her with Mr. Beshir Abdellatif, one of the Arab American candidates and a principal at another high school.

Now in its fourth year, KGIA is significantly under-enrolled, with only 109 students when it should have close to 200 students. Among the 109 students enrolled there are approximately 15 or fewer Arabic-speaking students. For the most part, many Arabic-speaking families have pulled their children out of the school for safety and transportation reasons. The school in this location is no longer a 6-12 grade school, but a middle school. It is no longer functioning as an Arabic dual-language school; it just offers Arabic as a foreign language. For the 2009-10 school year, KGIA received a C on the NYC Progress Report for poor student performance and progress in English Language Arts and math.

THE DANGEROUS DOMINANCE OF ISLAMOPHOBIA

In the last 4 years, I have gone through a lot professionally and personally in the public eye. I have learned a great deal about myself, my family, working for a bureaucratic institution, the politics of my city, and New Yorkers. I persevered, because of the love and support of my family and of complete strangers who saw my struggle as their own and gave me the will to battle an institution that many feared to challenge. The outcome of this experience was the EEOC ruling, which was a tremendous vindication.

Shortly after the ruling, I asked my lawyers to refrain from initiating additional litigation on the EEOC discrimination claim. I decided that it was time for me to move on with my professional and personal life. Additional litigation of the discrimination claim would mean reliving the unfortunate and painful events of August 6–10, 2007.

As I have affirmed before, I continue to be passionately committed to the school that my colleagues and I envisioned and proposed. I firmly believe that I have fulfilled my mission, which was to get KGIA approved and make sure it opened. I consider this a significant accomplishment.

While I have endured great injustice at the hands of people I trusted, especially the DOE, which has been my employer for 20 years, the far larger offense has been to the Arab and Muslim communities of the United States. In the years since 9/11, Arab and Muslim communities have been at the center of the most vile and hateful attacks. The attacks on me are part of a larger campaign to intimidate and silence marginalized communities. Among other strategies, the right wing is trying to coerce people from other communities to view Arabs and Muslims as threats to their safety and security.

What happened to me was a part of a growing trend of racism and bigotry against Arabs and Muslims in the United States. I was at the center of a political battle fueled by Islamophobia that goes beyond me as an individual to the intimidation of other Arabs and Muslims seeking to expand their role in U.S. public life. Islamophobia has dominated the media and Internet airwaves in the last several years; it sends the message that anything related to Arabs or Muslims is suspicious and frightening. Most recently in New York City, some critics of Park 51, the Islamic Center in downtown Manhattan, attacked it for being located "at Ground Zero" and thereby insensitive to the feelings of 9/11 families—as if *all* Muslims were responsible for 9/11. The Park 51 controversy exists within the context of other campaigns against the building of mosques and Islamic community centers in California, Illinois, New York, Tennessee, and Wisconsin, as well as graffiti, smashed windows, and arson at mosques across the country. Recently, in New York City, a Muslim cab driver was stabbed, and a verbal and physical bias attack was made on a Muslim teen in Staten Island by four of his classmates. Women like me who wear hijab have been harassed on the street and, in some instances, denied employment and refused entry to municipal courts in localities with a "no headgear" policy. Islamophobia was also prevalent in the 2008 presidential race when some of Barack Obama's opponents tied him to Islamic terrorists and insisted, despite ample evidence to the contrary, that he was a Muslim, as if that were a negative identity. Sadly, there are others who have been smeared or maligned as well, who have *not* been able to move on with their lives.

I have been fortunate to have the strength to draw on my experience to educate people about racism and bigotry. I am presently a part of Women Against Islamophobia & Racism (WAIR),[1] a New York City collective of educators, parents, and community activists from different ethnic, racial, and religious communities, which formed in response to the alarming growth of anti-Muslim sentiment and actions across the United States. Our aim is to challenge Islamophobia, racism, and xenophobia and connect struggles of identity-based discrimination. We have already begun to draw on our varied experiences and backgrounds as a way to link young people, educators, and organizers alike with curricular and other resources that will facilitate the creation of safe spaces, strong allies, and intentional communities.

As a U.S. citizen, as an educator, as a mother, as a sister, and a daughter, I want to ensure that what happened to me and other marginalized people doesn't continue to happen. I pledge to organize against Islamophobia and its impact on Arab and Muslim communities. I continue to dedicate my life to bridging the divides.

NOTE

1. WAIR also memorializes Thelma Jean Mothershed Wair for her bravery in taking a stand as a member of the Little Rock Nine, the African American students involved in the desegregation of Little Rock Central High School in 1957.

REFERENCES

Almontaser v. New York City Department of Education, 519 F.3d 505 (2nd Cir. 2008).

Debbie Almontaser v. New York City Department of Education and New Visions for Public Schools, EEOC Charge No. 520-2008-02337 (U.S. Equal Employment Opportunity Commission 2010).

Bennett, C., & Winter, J. (2007, August 6). City principal "revolting": Tied to 'intifada NYC' shirts." *New York Post*. Retrieved from http://www.nypost.com/p/news/regional/item_UerzwvF7fcSQY8YOP1ln4K

Cohler-Esses, L. (2007, August 17). Jewish shootout over Arab school." *The Jewish Week*. Retrieved from http://www.thejewishweek.com/features/jewish_shootout_over_arab_school

Colon, A. (2007, May 1). Arabic school idea is a monstrosity" *The New York Sun*. Retrieved from http://www.nysun.com/new-york/madrassa-plan-is-monstrosity/53557/

Elliott, A. (2010, March 12). Federal panel finds bias in ouster of principal. *The New York Times*. Retrieved from http://www.nytimes.com/2010/03/13/nyregion/13principal.html

Gootman, E. (2007, February 13). A new school plans to teach half of classes using Arabic. New York Times. Retrieved from http://www.nytimes.com/2007/02/13/nyregion/13schools.html?scp=1&sq=Khalil+Gibran+International&st=nyt

Pipes, D. (2007a, April 24). A madrassa grows in Brooklyn. *The New York Sun.* Retrieved from http://www.nysun.com/foreign/madrassa-grows-in-brooklyn/53060/

Pipes, D. (2007b, March 7). On New York's Khalil Gibran International Academy. *The New York Sun.* Retrieved from http://www.danielpipes.org/blog/2007/03/on-new-yorks-khalil-gibran-international

Rubinstein, D. (2007, March 10). Holy war! Slope parents protest arabic school plan. *The Brooklyn Paper* Retrieved from http://www.brooklynpaper.com/stories/30/11/30_11holywar.html

9

Social Justice High School

Truth and Transparency,
Community and Collective Power—
The Evolution of Social Justice High School

RITO MARTINEZ, WITH LISA ARRASTÍA

On Mother's Day in 2001, 14 Mexican mothers between the ages of 18 and 65 staged a 19-day hunger strike to demand a school for their children. The result of this multigenerational movement was the construction of a $63 million public high school complex. Every inch of the Little Village Lawndale High School campus was designed by the Chicago-based OWP/P Belluschi Architects together with the community of La Villita, or Little Village, which is located on Chicago's Southwest side. OWP/P describes the school site as a 280,000-square-foot:

> *1,400-student community high school [that] combines four small 350-student schools into one building. Based upon a universal creation myth, each school has a unique identity incorporating the elements of fire, earth, water and wind from Aztec mythology, which are cast as icons throughout their respective schools. In the central commons space, a solar calendar uses the reflection of the sun to commemorate the community's successful 19-day hunger strike, which was driven by the goal of providing new local school facilities. (n.d., online)*

Rito Martinez is the founding principal of Social Justice High School, one of the four small schools on the Little Village Lawndale campus.

* * * * * *

I think the story of Social Justice High School has to start and end with the community of La Villita and the hunger strike. The hunger strike was absolutely critical in forming the norms, values, and core beliefs of the school . . .

When I was thinking about applying to be the first principal of Social Justice High School, a lot of people from Chicago Public Schools (CPS) and even close friends thought I was absolutely crazy to even consider it. They said the school was doomed to fail because they felt there was absolutely no way that the school would ever be as powerful as the hunger strike. But I felt a commitment to the mothers of the strike and to my community, which Social Justice would serve, so I felt I had to do it.

There are so many leaders who are great, but then they leave their organizations and the organizations just crumble. I knew I didn't want to do that. From the very beginning, one of my mentors said, "The school can't be based on your charisma, Rito." That made so much sense to me, especially because of the hunger strike and how big it was as a grassroots struggle. Right from the start of fighting for and then building the school, I understood on a profound level that it would have to be the community values and strength of purpose on which the hunger strike was founded that would sustain the school, and not my leadership. I had the courage and the will to create something amazing, maybe not a school as powerful as the hunger strike, but still something very amazing. It was the belief in my own humility and the principles that the teachers and I came up with at our first retreat that kept me going.

At a retreat held the summer before the school opened in 2005, the teachers and I were struggling to define *social justice*. We were even questioning whether we should define it. We asked ourselves as educators how we might teach social justice. As the discussion continued, Noel Jones, a teacher, asked, "Well, why are we all here?" This question prompted us to share how we each became racially conscious, and when and how we became aware of power inequities in society and in our own lives. We really started sharing our hearts and our pain in terms of this journey. Out of all of our stories, we developed four core beliefs on which we based all school operations and interactions. They were truth and transparency; struggle and sacrifice; ownership and agency; and collective and community power.

Some of our teachers were already activists when they came to the school, and they had taught for 8, 10, and 12 years. They already had these core beliefs. Some had never really thought about issues of social justice, but they became socially conscious, and socially aware at the school through good old grassroots activism. I realized during our discussion that summer that the school was going to be about the collective vision of all teachers, students, and parents. I understood then that it was this vision that would sustain the actual work of opening and running the school.

To be sure, the core beliefs we designed very much governed and informed how we operated as a school; they impacted how we looked at discipline, how we looked at teacher leadership, and how we looked at decision making. But there were also specific events, some personal, others not, that occurred during the 4 years in which I was principal of Social Justice that for me reaffirmed something. As a school leader, starting and running a school entail great courage and personal sacrifice, but both are less difficult to carry out if energy is put in to develop a true working community where students, teachers, and parents feel a sense of ownership, have genuine leadership opportunities, and have the resources they need to unify, and take care of themselves and each other.

In the beginning of the school it was all about systems, core beliefs, and teacher, student, and parent ownership. . . .

We did a lot of things at first just because we were a small school. For example, we weren't allowed to have a Local School Council[1] (LSC) because the new rules from the state governing Small Schools—and these were definitely things pushed by Mayor Daley—mandated that Small Schools have advisory local school councils beginning in the third year of the school. These advisory councils don't have the full authority and power of LSCs. This meant that for the first couple of years we couldn't have any formal parent structures where parents could exercise some legitimate authority in the school like they can on LSCs.

It was important that parents not just be authentically involved, but also have authentic influence in the school. That's why we created a Parent Leadership Team. Of course, we could have relied on traditional methods for parent involvement like the PTA. There's also report card pick-up, sure. An awards assembly and you get some parent attendance, okay. Coming to school because your kid's in trouble. Or you can have these Parent Leadership Teams through which parents genuinely help to shape the school.

Once a year, we had parent walkthroughs, or "shadow days." This was a way for parents to maintain some of the formal authority they had lost because there wasn't an LSC. We would invite leadership team parents

and even the hunger strikers. They would measure things that were important to us and to them. Parents were responsible for answering questions
like: How do the hallways feel to you? Are kids respectful? Are they passing through the periods in a way that's conducive to their learning? Are
students engaged in classrooms? How are students feeling in terms of being in the cafeteria? How is the climate of the school when you're walking
in the building and interacting with students? We asked parents to help us
understand from *their* perspective what we needed to do to create a loving,
affirming educational environment.

During their walkthroughs, the parents would collect data in the
form of quotes and anecdotes. The teachers and I would chart and categorize what the parents observed and discovered. Together with parents, we would reflect on the data. Based on what we learned from the
information, changes and decisions were made. For instance, one question with which the parents wrestled was whether the students should
wear uniforms. Parents came to the walkthroughs. They saw the school
culture. They saw how the hallways, classrooms, and cafeteria operated
and felt. Comparing the same elements at three other schools, which had
uniforms, they saw that uniforms weren't making any difference. The
parents concluded that if kids are happier without uniforms, then we
shouldn't force the kids to wear them. The Parent Leadership Team and
interactive parent observations helped the school gain authentic parent
participation and enormous insight; they helped to strengthen our core
belief in and practice of truth and transparency.

*Being a Small School, what happens is you're not allowed to not see
the kids. . . .*

There's so much more demand for staff to respond to some of the socio-
emotional issues kids bring just so that we can support them academically.
In a large school, kids in desperate need can easily become invisible; they
can just disappear from school, literally. In a Small School, kids' needs are
magnified by 1,000% because you see and interact with them every day,
especially when the school becomes this external family, this place of well-
being for them. The kids are there right in front of you, screaming all the
time, "I need help!"

We were really fortunate because we had a Small Schools grant
through the Gates Foundation, which helped to augment our budget
quite a bit. Over 3 years, we received about $250,000. The money helped
us to do a lot of creative things to support the school's culture. What we
didn't have, though, were comprehensive social services, which the kids
and their families really needed.

In order to get some of the social services our kids needed, we worked with Enlace, which used to be Little Village Community Development Corporation. Enlace is an organization that works on economic development, violence prevention, and improving the quality of life for Little Village residents. Enlace partnered with Alivio and received a $400,000 start-up grant from Citgo Petroleum in order to install a health clinic on the Little Village Lawndale High School campus. Having the health clinic in the school impacted attendance tremendously, partly because kids could make appointments during the school day, during lunch; they could miss P.E. or one class to see the doctor instead of missing the entire day.

Even though the clinic was a huge support to the school, I still never felt like we had enough resources to deal with all of our kids who were homeless, wards of the state, or who had probation officers, highly dysfunctional families, and intense emotional needs. I also felt like we never had enough resources to deal with the other kind of social issues that our kids were bringing into the school. These were the important issues of race and class that impacted almost every aspect of their lives and their lives with us.

Ever since the school first opened in 2005, our black kids were getting beat up as they came to and from school on the CTA[2] bus. . . .

One of the major problems in our first year was that the bus stopped at Pulaski and 31st, which was six blocks from the school. The black kids were constantly being chased with bottles and pitbulls along 31st Street. Most of the people harassing the students weren't kids who attended Social Justice High School. They were kids between the ages of 15 and 21. Some of our African American students were in a rival black gang. When the black kids walked to school along 31st, it not only threatened rival gang turf but the gang's ability to keep black people, in general, out of the community.

Since the beginning, the vision of the school was about coalitions, solidarity, and uniting the African American and Latino communities. So, even as freshmen, black and Latino kids and teachers really organized to make a change in the CTA's bus route in order to provide our black kids with some safety. The students and teachers went to CTA board meetings and school board meetings in order to get CTA to extend the bus line at dismissal time so that our black kids wouldn't have to walk through rival gang territory to get to school. What the kids and teachers were asking was that the buses drop the kids off in front of the school. But CTA refused. CTA was more concerned with its "ridership."

After doing all that work in our first year, during the second year the kids and teachers became even more committed to the bus route project and the teachers integrated the project into their classes. This time, it worked. At dismissal time, students got two or three CTA buses to wait for them in front of the school every day so that our black kids could get out safely. Also, all the Latino kids who lived a little farther from the school and closer to North Lawndale could now take the bus. Of course, there was always some kid who would be like, "I'm not getting on the fucking bus! I'm walking down 31st" or "I'm walking down Kostner!" and then a conflict would ensue. Also, on occasion, the bus would get bricked or stuff would happen to it, but at least the kids were safe inside it.

Our son Sal was born. We were surprised and shocked. He had Down syndrome. . . .

In our second year, I told the school, "Guys, I really have to attend to my little boy." The staff was like, "Absolutely! Go tend to your son." And the school just kept going. And I thought, *Wow! All this work community building and developing teachers as leaders has really paid off.* While my wife and I were working to get Sal services, the teachers actually became the leaders of the school.

I was away for a good 6 weeks and there was no sort of issue in terms of student stability. Social Justice just kept going. For me, that was a great affirmation.

In the third year of the school, I learned I had a congenital heart defect. . . .

I had lived with this heart defect all my life and had no idea. I just knew that my heart would race sometimes, but the racing would eventually stop and I'd be fine. I guess I had learned how to, sort of, control it. But the stress was just building and building in the job. I'd get this really rapid heartbeat that wouldn't stop; it would last for hours and hours.

Finally, I went to the ER. They thought I was on drugs or something and they pumped me full of steroids. Steroids are supposed to decrease your heartbeat when you're high on cocaine or heroin, but they didn't do that for me because I wasn't high. If you can imagine this, my heart was pumping like 350, 400 beats per minute, which caused it to over-oxygenate my blood. My lungs got full of liquid and finally they collapsed and I began vomiting blood. I thought, *Oh my god, I'm going to die. I'm really going to die!*

So I'm in and out of consciousness and the doctors start to do the electric shocks on my heart with the paddles. After the third blast of the paddles, which was incredibly painful, my heart just sort of kicked back in to normal, and I was like, *Oh wow! I feel fine now.* It was as if they had hit a reset button. But then the steroids really started to kick in and my heart stopped. The doctors re-shocked me and I woke up in intensive care all tubed up. I had no idea what had happened.

All my life, I'd been living with this unexplained racing heart but within just a couple of hours in the ER, I found out that I have what's called Wolff-Parkinson-White syndrome. Basically, there were some extra nerve endings on top of my heart and they wanted to create their own rhythms by stealing electrical currents from the proper nerves. I'm fine now, but only after the doctors burned those extra nerves off.

My heart defect kept me away from the school for about 6 weeks. But once again, the school just continued.

At the beginning of my fourth year, a big black-brown race fight spilled out of the school at dismissal time and turned into hundreds of kids just fighting. . . .

Social Justice High School is located on the Southwest side of Chicago in South Lawndale, an area that includes the Mexican neighborhood known as Little Village. The school is 11 blocks from Cermak Road, which divides South from North Lawndale. North Lawndale is mostly black and there are times when Little Village is extremely anti–African American. It's always been that way. Under Illinois' desegregation consent decree, the CPS Capital Planning Group delineated the boundaries for the four schools of which Social Justice is a part, which meant that about 30% of the school's seats were set aside for students from North Lawndale. Some of the Latino community was so angry that the boundaries did not include more of Little Village, because in their minds Social Justice wouldn't end up being the Latino school they had imagined. As a result, there was community and political opposition. I knew we couldn't start a school in this way and I demonstrated my opposition to this resistance. When we opened the school, in the local newspaper there was a cartoon of me holding up a big barrier and I was escorting black kids into the school and keeping Latino kids out.

State senator Martin Sandoval was really angry. He was like, "the boundaries have to be redrawn and you have to include more Latino kids." He basically said, "We don't want African American kids." Sandoval even proposed a referendum asking CPS to have the boundaries redrawn so that the school would mostly include kids from Little Village. Community organizations like Instituto del Progreso Latino, Lawndale Christian Development Corporation, and Little Village Community Development Corporation, some parents, and I opposed the referendum. We stood up for the school's potential to unify blacks and Latinos in the community. I wrote a letter to the editor questioning the intent of the referendum. I explained that the school's value was in its unity, and although it was unfortunate that we couldn't have more students enrolled from Little Village, I argued the answer was not to keep African American kids out. Sandoval immediately demanded that I get fired. He went to Mayor Daley and Arne Duncan. He just wanted my head for calling him a racist. In the end, kids from Little Village and kids from North Lawndale attended the school together, but not always happily.

At our first parent meeting, there was a lot of outreach into North Lawndale. African American and Latino parents all came together at this big potluck at which I shared my belief that the adults in the community have to model what we want from our kids. I asked the parents to work collectively. We continued to meet once a month, and even met in each other's churches and homes one time. We shared food, stories, and our values. Whenever there were racial issues in the school, I always included the voices of parents. In this way, there were always Latino and African American parents showing their kids how they could be united.

Despite the efforts of some of the African American and Latino parents, though, we still always had tons of racial tensions and fights. Often, the fights were over something silly like some girl and some boy in an interracial relationship, but sometimes, like this one day in February 2009, one of the fights turned into something much larger.

We had always been very active being outside the school during arrival and dismissal times to try to ensure safe passage for all of our students, several of whom were crossing gang lines just to attend the school. But this one time, our vigilance was matched. All my staff was outside the school and we were getting kids on buses. Teachers were getting kids to stop fighting and asking them to go home. Then the police came with paddy wagons and they exacerbated the tensions. They were telling the black kids "If you don't want this to happen, then go to Manley.[3] Get out of this community! This is your fault this is happening to you!" The cops were just being complete racist assholes; they were manhandling kids and almost making things worse.

Teachers were outside the school trying to get kids on buses while the fight was going on. At the same time, I was dealing with parents and questions. At around 4:30 or 5:00, when the fight had calmed down some, the assistant principal and I tried to address the concerns of parents, directing relatives to hospitals, submitting the proper reports, and trying to figure out, *All right, what do we do tomorrow when the kids come back?* But the entire staff, 35 Social Justice teachers, drove to the police station and demanded to speak with the commander because they were concerned and angry about the conduct of the police officers. They all walked into the police station and they all collectively got kicked out. The police told them that they would only speak to two teachers. The teachers were very respectful and still demanded to speak to the commander. He finally came out and took all the teachers into a large community room. Two teachers served as spokespeople. They detailed how inappropriate the police were. And, by the way, they videotaped all of this. The police actually let them videotape the whole conversation.

So, there were some good things that came out of the fight. The police apologized. The commander was extremely complimentary to the teachers about how active they were in ensuring students' safety. He volunteered his officers to come to the school to talk to groups of kids to describe riot control, to explain to them how to work with the police in situations like this and how not to make the situations worse. But like with the bussing problem in our first year, the question of who was responsible for student and school safety remained an issue in our fourth year.

Subsequent to the fight, we had a huge town hall meeting with Huberman and all stakeholders. The town hall meeting worked really well, but helping our kids process all of this was difficult, incredibly profound, and positive. Having that video of the teachers speaking with the police commander and showing it to the entire student body was really powerful; it really helped the students understand the context of, again, social justice, fighting oppression, fighting power, fighting racism, and how complex it all is. Showing the students how their teachers had spent 4 or 5 hours into the night beyond their own work schedules to advocate for them really meant something to the kids. They saw that we weren't just sitting on our hands as they were being, in many ways, violated by the city supposedly there to protect them.

Historically, the divide between African Americans and Latinos in this country has been wide and long. You know how they say that carving a path in stone takes a long time? Well, maybe it won't actually take too long because at Social Justice we ourselves were enacting our core belief in collective and community power. The teachers went down to that station for the black kids *and* the Latino kids, and the teachers didn't ask, "Rito, can we go down to the station?" They just did it. They took action, acted as leaders, and said we have to do something about this issue. That's confirmation, a reaffirmation that the values of Social Justice were actually driving the school and not necessarily my own leadership.

By the beginning of the 2009–2010 school year, I was already under investigation for residency violation. . . .

As of 1996, Chicago principals had to live within the city's limits. When I first started the school in 2005, I lived in Chicago, but Letty, who was my fiancée at the time, lived in a house in Oak Park, which is just on the outskirts of the city. Letty, who was then an assistant principal at Little Village Academy, was exempt from the residency requirement because she'd been hired before 1996.[4] When we got married, we did consider moving back to the city. But I didn't want to displace Letty; she had worked so hard to buy this little home in Oak Park. So I moved to Oak Park instead.

I told both of my supervisors, "Look, I have two residencies. I have my address with CPS where my mom lives in Chicago and I live in Oak Park with my family." I helped my mom with the rent so I even had rent receipts that proved I kind of lived there. I was always really up front with my supervisors, but they always said the law says wherever you intend to go back to sleep every night is your residency. Be careful.

It was in year two of the school when Letty and I really began contemplating, *Do we sell? Do we rent? Do we go back into the city?* For a couple of thousand dollars, we even hired a lawyer to see if we could get the exemption extended to include marriages that occurred after 1996. The lawyer made inquiries at CPS's law department without using our names. After a year, the information from the legal department came back saying, "No. You absolutely cannot extend the policy through marriage. You'll just have to move your entire family into Chicago."

Then Sal was born. At first, we didn't know that Sal had Down syndrome. And we definitely didn't know that at 4 months old he would need open-heart surgery to repair his heart. Once we began learning about Sal's disAbility, we also began to understand that *Oh, we're parents of a special needs child. He's going to need physical therapy, occupational therapy, developmental therapy, speech therapy, and he's going to need all of these therapies at 6 months old! And oh, all of this will have to be delivered in the home but we're both working, and* . . . It was a lot to learn in a short amount of time, and it was a really difficult time.

But we still kept debating whether we should move into the city or stay in Oak Park. We did research into social service agencies that provide services for kids with special needs in the city of Chicago. We found out there's a one- to two-year waiting list to get physical therapists to come to your home, and a one- to two-year waiting list for developmental therapists as well as all of the other services that Sal and our family would need. We called all around Oak Park and social service agencies were like, "Sure, we'll be there next week." We decided we'd no longer even struggle with the decision of going back to the city. I was going to do the best that I could for my little boy and there was no way I was having my family leave Oak Park. So I took my chances with CPS.

The August right before the school's fourth year, which was 2008, I got this anonymous, very hate-filled, threatening email from somebody saying, "I know you don't actually live in the city of Chicago and I'm going to turn you in to the inspector general." Devastated, I said to myself, *All right, there goes the plan.*

I went to the law department at CPS and told them, "Look, guys, this is what's going on. I got this email. I'm in violation. I've tried not to lie and I'm not going to lie." I told them that I had a lot of documentation proving that I had sought legal counsel on this. Legal said, "Okay, well, you're going to be under investigation and then you have to go through the proper procedure." I was then under surveillance for a while.

Later, there was a hearing. My lawyer told me, "Whatever you do, don't lie, because if you lie, they'll immediately fire you."

The first question they asked at the hearing was "Do you live at this address in Oak Park?"

"Yes, I live at this address."

"What color is your dog?"

And I'm like, "My dog? My dog is tan."

"What time does your babysitter get to your home?"

"About 6:00 in the morning."

They had so many particular questions about the details that occur in and around my home. It was really, really eerie.

I talked to CPS around December, a couple of months after the hearing. I told them that I had no intention of moving back to Chicago. I explained that I would love to finish the year so that I'd have a chance to be intentional with leading the transition to another principal. They told me to finish the year and make my resignation effective June 30.

April comes around and it's a Tuesday. It's about 4 months after I thought everything was settled. I get this phone call from one of the city's newspapers. The reporter says something like this:

"Isn't it ironic, Mr. Martinez, that you're the Social Justice principal, but you're lying about your residency?"

"You know, I've always been very up front about everything with CPS, but I don't want to go into my personal life with *you*."

"Well, I'm going to run a story anyway on how the Social Justice principal is a liar and has lied about his residency."

"I guess you're going to do what you're going to do. I could tell you the story of my personal decisions regarding this process off the record, or I could tell you on the record. Either way, none of this has been easy."

Then I'm scrambling because the story's going to come out on Friday, so I had to call a special assembly for Thursday. I had to bring all my kids into the auditorium and tell them what was happening.

"I have to be truthful with you and I have to apologize to you because you don't deserve the kind of attention that this school is going to get. You don't deserve this disruption." It was just absolutely devastating to the kids. Students and teachers were crying.

I had really wanted to be intentional and wait for the right timing in terms of the transition in leadership, but on Friday in the newspaper, they print a photograph of both homes, my mom's and my family's, and she just runs this horrible story. Both Latino news channels and every local network news program ran something like "Star Principal in CPS Living a Lie." It was a complete exposé that destroyed me publicly.

Despite the way the news of my residency violation came out and the way I had to rush to tell the school, the kids and teachers were extremely supportive; everyone was involved in the transition plan.

The transition planning was powerful and the search process was lengthy. I worked really hard at generating community participation. I begged and forced Manuelita[5] and Toby, another hunger striker who had a couple of kids in the school, to take days off of work and put in 8–10 hours a day to go through every single résumé for a principal in order to make the selection process extremely transparent, especially because CPS was just hyper about making sure that we followed all procedures to the letter. The advisory local school council, which included members of the community, parents, and students, were all on the interview committee. Everyone was involved in finding the kind of new principal who shared and could sustain the core values of the school, values we had just spent 4 years living and exemplifying.

Although the search was really intensive, the transition process itself was really smooth. The community chose my assistant principal, Chad Weiden, to lead the school. Their confidence in Chad says something about the authentic collective the school built over the years I was there; it was a community where people could be truthful and transparent about who they are. Chad is a young, gay, white man and the community chose him to lead this school of Latino and African American children. African American and Latino families love and embrace Chad because he shares with them the values of truth and transparency, community and collective power, and struggle and sacrifice.

Today, the parents are involved in the school and the kids are passionate about their own education and improving their community. Scores are decent. Attendance is consistently at 95%. College acceptance and scholarships are off the charts. In fact, in 2006, Roosevelt University provided a scholarship covering the tuition of our 2009 and 2010 graduates who qualify for admission.[6] That's an offer worth over $35,000 per student per year. In 2009, eight students won the Roosevelt scholarship.

Student activism has also produced major accomplishments. For example, students studied nutrition and student lunches. They presented their findings to the school board, pressured the catering company to change its practices, then pressured CPS to resist renewing the catering contract unless the menu changed. The students gained healthy options for CPS kids citywide. In their efforts to demonstrate unity between Little Village and North

Lawndale, the students studied the federal desegregation decree. They testi-fied at the federal hearing where CPS argued that it no longer discriminates against students of color. According to the judge hearing the case, our stu-dents were the first group of students to ever testify in a federal case involv-ing education. The students also organized a citywide student walkout in response to teacher and education budget cuts. These are just the major events that got press last year.

And me, well, in April of my last year at Social Justice High School, I started looking frantically for a job. Absolutely nobody would hire me because of the political risk that the press around the violation produced. That was painful. But I got really blessed and found a great position working with the Network for College Success at University of Chicago. We're sort of the prac-tice arm for the university's Consortium on Chicago School Research.

Although the school operated and continues to operate with a deep commitment to the core beliefs we created during that first summer retreat, I think the story of how the school started and my time as its principal pro-vide powerful examples of the ways in which truth and transparency, strug-gle and sacrifice, ownership and agency, collective and community power were all put into practice. Throughout my time at the school, I learned that the implementation of and fidelity to a school's core beliefs could give life to a school. In this way, Social Justice High School continues to do its work in honor of the hunger strike. It doesn't matter that the school will never be able to outdo the hunger strike. What's important is that social justice is in action through the life of the entire school.

NOTES

1. In Chicago, schools that are not alternative or small schools have LSCs or local school councils. Made up of parents, teachers, community members, and a school's principal, LSCs approve the distribution of funds and resources, develop and oversee the annual school improvement plan, as well as evaluate and oversee a school's principal. LSCs are often a place where parents and community members can have tremendous influence on the operations of their children's school.

2. Chicago Transit Authority.

3. In 2009, Social Justice High School's student body was 75% Latino and 23% Af-rican American, whereas Manley Career Academy High School's student body was 99% African American. Chicago Public Schools allowed Social Justice to commit to a small school design, which meant that in 2009 it maintained an enrollment of 385 students and an average class size of 20 students. The same was not true for Manley, which enrolled 1,102 students and maintained an average class size of almost 24 students per class. See the "2009 Illinois School Report Card" at http://schools2009.chicagotribune.com/.

4. In 1996, the Chicago School Board permitted those city employees hired between September 1, 1980, and August 26, 1996, who resided outside the city of Chicago, to continue living outside the city, but it required all new employees to be city residents.

5. Manuelita García is known as the matriarch of the hunger strike movement. When the hunger strike began, she was its eldest member, at 65 years old. Manuelita currently serves on the Social Justice Advisory Local School Council and she is still very active in the school and community. The school dedicated a mural in her honor called the "Wall of Hope." She is the central figure in the mural and she has her arms open, embracing and protecting images of the school and students.

6. On October 31, 2006, the *Chicago Sun-Times* reported that in order to qualify, Social Justice students must complete an AP (Advanced Placement) or other college preparatory course; score 20 or above on the ACT college admission exam; and graduate high school with a 3.0 or above grade-point average. In addition, Roosevelt's scholarship will only cover the amount of tuition that state and federal aid do not. See also *Roosevelt University News and Events*, June 6, 2009, at http://www.roosevelt.edu/News_and_Events/News_Articles/20090609-SJHS.aspx.

REFERENCE

OWP/P Cannon Design. (n.d.) Little Village High School, Chicago, IL. Retrieved from http://www.owpp.com/content.cfm/little_village_high_school

10

High School for Recording Arts

Old School, New School

DAVID "TC" ELLIS, WITH SAM SEIDEL

> Black man, you don't have to bash white people. All we've got
> to do is go back home and turn our communities into productive
> places.
>
> —Minister Louis Farrakhan

I had no plan on going to the Million Man March at all. I got roped into it by my old mentor, Bobby Hickman. I was trying not to go, but Bobby just said, "I'm gonna come pick you up tomorrow."

When we got to Washington, DC, the energy was incredible. We went to the hotel and quickly decided not to even stay there. We went right to the National Mall and camped out. I remember in the morning when I woke up and the sun was rising and there was just a sea of people coming in like water flowing into a lake.

We weren't probably 100 feet away from where Farrakhan and different people were coming to speak. Farrakhan had a strong message for us to go back to our communities and do something that was healing, something that was going to be supportive of our community and people in general. He really kept it all human. It wasn't all about race and being black; it was more about being a positive human being and doing something constructive in whatever community you were in.

Not long before the march, I finished a run as a rapper and recording artist. I had been signed to Warner Brothers Records and toured with Prince, but had recently returned to St. Paul, Minnesota, and opened a recording studio downtown. All these kids, mostly young black men, kept hanging around my studio during the day. I'd ask them why they weren't at school. They'd tell me that school was wack and that what they wanted to do was learn how to make money off making music. They wanted to learn, but just didn't have the right avenues. The march was a confirmation of what I was already thinking in my mind about what I needed to do. The whole van ride back to St. Paul I was talking about how I wanted to start a school. Bobby kept checking me, "What you're trying to do ain't easy, it's a lot of work."

I respected Bobby and I was listening to him, but I was just blissed out. Sometimes I believe ignorance is bliss, because, honestly, if I had known about all the compliance issues and everything that goes along with operating a school, I probably wouldn't have been able to do what I did. Knowing what I know now, I probably never would have started High School for Recording Arts. But at that time, nothing Bobby said could deter me. I listened to him, but I had an instinct that had been following me and I had to follow it.

I began enlisting others who I knew could strengthen my vision and help transform it into reality. I reached out to past mentors, such as Bobby, who had run youth programs. One important reconnection I made at that time was Dr. Wayne Jennings, who was my principal from the St. Paul Open School, the alternative high school from which I graduated 20 years earlier.

Dr. Jennings had founded another school nearby, the St. Paul Family Learning Center, and he was thrilled to see me interested in continuing the legacy of providing alternatives for students who, like myself, rejected or were rejected by the mainstream. Most of these students come from chaotic family systems and communities. They arrive hungry, angry, without socially acceptable coping skills, and behind in school credits.

Dr. Jennings suggested that we make my studio a pilot recording arts education program as a satellite of the St. Paul Family Learning Center. He had received a charter from the Minnesota State Department of Education to operate a K–12 charter school. However, it was set up to start with just the youngest students and then grow over a period of years. We went to the state and requested that they approve an acceleration of the school's staggered grade introduction schedule. This allowed us to operate as a satellite of the St. Paul Family Learning Center and made it possible for me to hire our first teacher.

Our initial curriculum was based on the newspaper. In addition to teaching students how to make and sell music, every day we taught social studies, language arts, and science through that day's edition of the *St. Paul Dispatch*. But with Dr. Jennings sharing his perspective from 50 years in the education game, our approach quickly expanded to incorporate multiple strategies.

Dr. Jennings pulled on his experience in schools and his educational research—he has hundreds of articles published—to help me design the academic program for the school. We incorporated project-based learning, direct instruction, hands-on experiences, community service, an advisory model, and more. It was really a by-any-means-necessary approach to education. Dr. Jennings's encyclopedic knowledge of educational practices presented me with the perfect catalog of educational models from which to devise a unique blend customized specifically for our students.

Because we were pulling on so many different educational techniques, we developed a framework for assessing students that focused on validating competency instead of just awarding credits for seat time. We created a set of 12 HSRA Validations (High School for Recording Arts) that incorporated areas in which we wanted all students to be competent by the time they graduated. These are competencies we still use now. The validations include areas such as Science and Technology, Literary Analysis, and Accessing Information, which align to state standards; as well as Community Involvement and Philosophical, Emotional, and Spiritual Awareness, which are areas that, although not state standards, align with our community values.

While I was receiving educational support on these and other academic developments from Dr. Jennings, I turned to others for assistance with developing the music program and facilities. I saw that the music had a powerful ability to attract students and engage them. Students who wouldn't focus long on anything else could go deep if I got them in front of some equipment.

So I began trying to supplement my existing studio, but we ran into challenges finding the funds for everything required. Meanwhile, a younger nephew-cousin of mine had a gangsta rap crew who had built an impressive studio. Eventually, they lost their studio space and he offered some of the equipment to me. It was too good to be true, and indeed, there was a catch: My nephew-cousin did not want his crew's legacy to die. He said the studio would have to take on the name of their gangsta rap group, "Down 4 Dirt."

I told him, "You know I'm not down with no 'Down 4 Dirt.'"

And he was like, "Ain't there no way we can keep the '4' alive?"

"If we can keep the equipment, we can keep the '4' alive. . . ." I told him. "We'll make it 'Studio 4.'" This made it possible for me to assemble a high-quality recording studio for my students, without carrying on any negative legacy from Down 4 Dirt.

In addition to gaining the equipment, a relationship was sparked with a talented songwriter and producer, Philip Winden. Winden had been doing production and engineering work for Down 4 Dirt and I was introduced to him by my nephew-cousin. We discovered that we had known each other many years earlier through a mutual friend.

Initially, I hired Phil to help get the new studio equipment hooked up properly. I realized I needed someone with engineering expertise and Phil quickly became an indispensable part of the program, as chief engineer and producer. Phil was a hands-on learner who had a lot of the same issues with traditional education as me, and as the students I intended to serve. None of us thrived in environments based on direct "sage on the stage" instruction. We preferred the "guide on the side" approach.

Phil didn't judge kids at all based on their academic proficiency. He zeroed in on students' talents. If a young person couldn't spell, Phil would quickly find out what the young person was good at and he would help accentuate it. In this way, even though Phil wasn't a certified teacher, he set an example for our whole staff, by demonstrating how powerful it is to really treat young people with respect. Once students caught the vibe in the studio with Phil, we could get them hooked into lots of other projects. We have strived to make that energy permeate throughout the school ever since.

Beyond the important aspect of getting the studio built and running, there were many other new challenges that arose while transforming a private recording studio into a public school. We had to familiarize ourselves with reams of regulations specific to school operations, implement new reporting systems, and make facilities improvements.

We had very little money to fix up our space. I had an innate entrepreneurial sense, but I had never written a grant—so I went to the richest guy I knew: Wolfie.

Wolfie was a hoodstar. He drove a souped-up Cadillac Coupe De Ville and had tremendous street credibility. He was naturally good with money and was a friend I knew I could trust and depend on. Wolfie loved the idea of being a part of a recording studio and school. He signed on to using his creative hustle mentality to help make it a reality.

Wolfie's partners would give him a hard time about pouring his time and resources into his newfound passion. They'd come at him like, "You're takin' a bath on that studio," and he'd be like, "If you wanna get cleaned up, you gotta take a bath." Being a part of the school start-up was Wolfie's way of moving away from street economics and into building a supportive institution for young people.

While I operated by common sense, Wolfie had an intense eye for the regulations and formalities of the system. He was great with paperwork. The same intelligence he was known for in the street came in handy organizing binder books of education procedures and compliance regulations from the district. He'd be like, "Look, you need to show the fire department this right here." He was obsessed with playing everything strictly by the book. This became a guiding influence on the school's administrative culture, and Wolfie's level of diligence remains our standard to this day.

Wolfie also had such a thorough reputation in the street that, until leukemia claimed his life, his presence at the school rendered discipline issues virtually nonexistent. If there was a problem, there was no one in the streets he couldn't reach out to and get it resolved. Wolfie would come in on some students acting up like, "What . . . are you doing?" And that was the end of it. He just was not challenged.

The way Wolfie's street connects improved school safety was another lesson we have carried from the early days of HSRA. In subsequent years, I followed Wolfie's lead by reaching out to gang leaders, helping to coordinate a truce, and negotiating the High School for Recording Arts as a known neutral zone among local gangs.

A lot of people probably would have cut off their street affiliations as soon as they decided to start a school. Instead, I tried to flip those relationships into resources that could help create and run the school. Without my nephew-cousin's equipment and Wolfie's help, I couldn't have built the school in the literal brick-and-mortar sense. Without Wolfie's presence and sensibilities, I would not have been as successful at appealing to or working effectively with kids from the 'hood.

After a couple of years of building up the school's resources and programs as a satellite of the St. Paul Family Learning Center, Dr. Jennings suggested to me that we write a charter application to incorporate the High School for Recording Arts as its own institution.

The first teacher who built a relationship with me as a student at St. Paul Open School, Joe Nathan, had become a national expert on school reform. He understood how the Minnesota State Department of Education worked and he advised us throughout the application process. We wrote the charter application over a period of about a month and a half and, once it was approved by the state, Dr. Jennings began serving as superintendent of the school and as chair of the school's board. In these capacities, he made it his mission to help protect the school from district personnel, state-level bureaucrats, foundation program officers, and teachers who were set in their traditional ways—all of whom have tried to force the school to take on a more traditional academic program rather than our radical, experiential, project- and competency-based approach. This was an especially large issue in the early days, before we had established our model and proven its success.

At the time, around 1998, the charter approval process was open to innovative newcomers and was much less bureaucratic than it is now. Nevertheless, the Minnesota Department of Education meeting at which the school's charter was approved was a great moment in my life and immediately brought encouraging attention to our work.

That attention carried new challenges and opportunities along with it. For instance, when the charter was approved, a newspaper reporter came around asking what the "4" in Studio 4 represented. In my head, I was like, "Damn, it came from 'Down 4 Dirt,'" but that was when I got blessed. Off the top of my head I told her, "Well, that's family, respect, community, and education."

Surely, there can be some risk and lost opportunities that come with such spontaneity. Many schools or organizations would have had a series of meetings to identify the core values of their community. Surveys would have gone out, results would have been measured and discussed, decision-making methods would have been agreed upon. In this way, they would have ensured a thorough selection process with broad buy-in from everyone involved. But I didn't have time for a series of meetings. I was taking Down 4 Dirt equipment and repurposing it for our positive mission. The newspaper reporter had put me on the spot and I needed a socially acceptable answer for the name of the studio. I looked into my heart, pulled on the improvisational wordplay skills that I had honed as a rapper, and trusted that what came out would be right. The article was glowing and the school continued growing. I have never regretted making such an important decision in the spur of the moment. It was the perfect building block we needed at the time. The staff and students instantly took to it, and to this day, *Family*, *Respect*, *Community*, and *Education* stand strong as the pillars of our school community.

I realize now that that spontaneous style is part of our school's essence. The experimentation is very important to the viability and attraction of the school. If the intent is good and the work is good, let some things come about as they may. Then again, other aspects of school leadership and growth needed to be more carefully orchestrated. For this, I needed more strong educators who shared my ideals and could help shape the academic and administrative components of the school. Paula Anderson was an English teacher and an academic coordinator at an Alternative Learning Program in the area. She had also been a teacher at the St. Paul Open School. I met her at an Art Crawl in Downtown St. Paul, and in talking with her about my vision for High School for Recording Arts, I found that she had experience operationalizing some of the curricular and assessment strategies I hoped to implement.

When I was an aspiring rap artist, I would approach Prince, whom I knew from growing up in St. Paul. Every time I saw him, I would push him to give me a chance to record and perform with him. I pursued Paula in the same way. Every time I saw her, I would ask her to work at the High School for Recording Arts. At first, she refused, so I would pay her $50 to

come by and talk to our staff about the idea of competency-based graduation plans, which had become an area of expertise for Paula through her
position at the Alternative Learning Program. As Paula spent time at our
school through her sporadic visits, she came to see it as a place that not
only permitted but fostered innovation. A school where there was no box
to have to think outside of.

Having hosted a punk rock radio show in college, Paula wasn't a hip-
hop head, but she understood the power of music. As she grew to appreciate what a unique environment the High School for Recording Arts was,
the Prince treatment prevailed and Paula came to work at the school as our
academic director.

When it came to the business aspects of running the studio and school,
such as selecting a location, soliciting donations, or negotiating contracts,
I always had a lot of confidence. Sometimes my style came across as brash.
I would show up to meetings and speak from my heart, but some people
could not hear my message through my street vernacular, or else they were
put off by my baggy attire. Rather than pretend to be someone I'm not, I realized I needed a smooth counterpart. As long as someone had on a suit and
tie, I could keep wearing my hoody and gold chain. I had met an entertain-
ment lawyer named Tony Simmons through my time in the music business.
We initially hit it off at a music conference on the east coast, but Tony had
family in Minnesota, so whenever he'd come out, I would get him to come
by the school and give seminars to students on the business of music.

When it came time for the school's charter to be reviewed, I was confident about what needed to be said. But I asked Tony to come out and help
with how to say it. I knew I was likely to offend someone and I wanted a
sharp lawyer rolling with me. Tony was like an extreme other side of me.
Our relationship struck a perfect balance, because Tony has equal respect
for my style and quickly fell in love with the philosophy of the school.

High School for Recording Arts never would have come into existence if it weren't for the absolute conviction and clarity I felt coming
out of the Million Man March. But it also wouldn't have happened if I
had not been willing to reach out to and learn from my old high school
principal, Dr. Wayne Jennings; a white woman who'd hosted a punk rock
radio show in college, Paula Anderson; and a pretty-boy lawyer from
New York City, Tony Simmons.

I have relied on this team to combine all of their skills and strengths to
build the school. But in other instances, when, as the founder, I have seen a
need to flip the script and do something that hasn't been done before, I have
had to maintain my conviction—even when my valued team of collaborators
did not see eye-to-eye with me. This occurred when we were transitioning

from running a for-profit recording studio to running an educational program. I wanted to continue running the studio as a for-profit company and have the school contract the studio to provide programming. Initially, Tony, who's an attorney; my ex-wife, who's also an attorney; and another guy who was the business manager told me we couldn't do that. They all told me, "It's a conflict of interest. Make up your mind, either you wanna be a for-profit company or you're gonna be a nonprofit, and really you've gotta be a nonprofit because you want to start a school!" But I refused to file the papers that would dissolve the for-profit business and incorporate it as a nonprofit organization. A few weeks later, Tony came across an article in the *New York Times* about an emerging trend of for-profits and nonprofits contracting with each other. This precedent convinced all the naysayers. They prepared the paperwork and I got my way. That was something I had learned from working with Prince—to stand my ground. I didn't want to give up the autonomy of having my own company, so I didn't.

Having a privately held business own and operate the recording studio within the school allowed for a type of flexibility uncommon for schools. For instance, students could record uncensored music after hours, without it having been made on equipment owned by the school district. On the other hand, the school's nonprofit status saves taxes and enables us to apply for grants and receive donations. What we're doing is a hybrid, and it gives us an opportunity to accomplish things more efficiently.

The same team that I pushed around the school's dual status came together with me to tackle our first major political challenge. At the 3-year review of our charter, which took place around the beginning of the millennium, one of the compliance officers who was part of the review process claimed that the school was inaccurately reporting attendance and enrollment and he estimated that the school owed the state over $150,000. This sparked negative attention from the local media. A leading state lawmaker was reported as having said something like, "There goes another charter that won't be opening its doors next year." The next thing we knew, we were undergoing an audit by the Minnesota State Department of Education and subsequently another audit by the IRS.

This tore at the fiber of our community. Students, staff members, and families thought the school would be denied a charter renewal and would be forced to close. I couldn't understand why this was happening to us—we were doing everything by the book! My lawyer said I should buy a lotto ticket because in all his years he had never seen a 501(c)(3) get audited and here we were, in 1 year, being audited by three entities. Finally the audits were completed. And guess what? It turned out the state had underpaid us for our enrollment and they *owed us* $5,000!

But the St. Paul Public School board was still giving us trouble and threatening not to renew our charter. In the final approval meeting for the charter renewal, one of the board members said, "Wait a minute, I think we need to recognize that this school is doing something we haven't been able to accomplish." Speaking of our student population—which includes at least a third who have been homeless in any given year, 67% that have been involved with the criminal justice system, and 91% that receive free and reduced lunch—he said, "They are reaching students who we have not been successful serving."

This was a turning point. Not just in the charter renewal process—though it did lead the haters on the board to acquiesce and approve our renewal—but also in our school's history. It wasn't that it was the only serious challenge we would face, but it taught us that as long as we continued to do great work with students, we could survive.

It is now 2010. The charter review ordeal was 10 years ago and the trials and tribulations have continued to this day. This year, we have spent hundreds of hours battling with the Minnesota State Department of Education, who were trying to categorize our school as "persistently low-achieving" based on our 4-year graduation rate. This was a totally unfair designation, given that they calculate the rate from when students first started high school and our mission is to serve students who have come to us after several years of no or low credit attainment at other high schools. Our average student is 17.6 years old and enters our school at least 1.6 years behind in credits. We move students through as quickly as we can, but we cannot in good conscience graduate students before they are ready—and many of our students arrive without enough time to be prepared to graduate within 4 years of the first day they set foot in high school.

Eventually, after frequent trips to the state capitol to engage directly with the Minnesota Department of Education; communication with and visits to the U.S. Department of Education; numerous conversations with state legislators, education policy experts, and lawyers; and drafting a bill amendment, they removed us from the "low-achieving" list. But once again, our entire community had to have fortitude and come together to endure negative press and outside evaluators looking for any cracks they could find in our programs. Luckily, now we have a generation of graduates and a pile of wonderful articles and awards to affirm the work we do.

Sometimes I think back on our van ride home to Minnesota from the Million Man March; the feeling I had inside me that day, the clarity and confidence I felt about my mission to start a school for young people who didn't fit in the traditional system. I had already seen the need and felt the passion, but my experience in DC gave me inspiration and conviction. My mission with High School for Recording Arts is to create experiences like that for as many young people as possible.

As much as we want to prepare our students for every possible scenario they might find themselves in, we have to remember to not always educate them to the complexities of everything that they're trying to do, because when we do that, we make the dream impossible. Sometimes when you don't know all the limitations, it gives you the power to do what you want to do. All you see is the goal and you don't have enough sense not to try it. You go for it, and you make it, and that's what happened to me.

About the Contributors

Debbie Almontaser is the founding and former principal of the Khalil Gibran International Academy. As a 20-year veteran of the New York City public school system, she taught special education, inclusion, trained teachers in literacy, and served as a multicultural specialist and diversity advisor. She is a founding board member of The Dialogue Project and a member of the board of directors of Women in Islam. She is also co-founder of Brooklyn Bridges, the September 11th Curriculum Project, and We Are All Brooklyn.

Lisa Arrastía has been teaching and leading creative educational programs in independent, public, and charter schools for almost 20 years. She is the middle school principal at United Nations International School, and the founder and former director of City as Classroom School in Chicago. Currently a candidate for the Ph.D. in American studies at University of Minnesota, her research interests are the contemporary education economy, the iconographies of difference in education, and the geography of education. Lisa has won several teaching and research awards, among them an American Association of University Women and a New Leaders for New Schools fellowship. Her work in the classroom is the focus of an Emmy-nominated PBS documentary, *Making the Grade*. Originally from New York City, Lisa lives in New York City with her husband Mark Nowak and their 10-year-old daughter.

Ann Cook is co-founder and co-director of Urban Academy High School and co-chair of the New York Performance Standards Consortium, a coalition of New York State Schools that has developed and implemented a performance-based system of assessment in lieu of high-stakes testing. She has taught at Sarah Lawrence, Brooklyn, and Queens Colleges has written numerous articles on educational reform, schools, and teaching, and is the author of several children's books, including *Meet Monster*. She is the parent of three children who graduated from New York City public schools.

David Domenici is co-founder of the See Forever Foundation, chair of its board, and a founding board member of the Maya Angelou Public Charter School. He is the director of the Center for Educational Excellence at the University of Maryland.

David "TC" Ellis is the founder and director of High School for Recording Arts, also known as "Hip Hop High." The school received a charter from the Minnesota Department of Education and has emerged as the only public school of its kind in the United States. David is a graduate of the St. Paul Open School. He established himself in the music business in the mid-1980s as the first rap recording artist to release a record in Minnesota, and he was eventually recruited by Prince and Warner Brothers to record and produce records at Paisley Park. David currently lives in the Twin Cities, where he was born and raised.

James Forman Jr. is co-founder of the See Forever Foundation, Maya Angelou Public Charter School, and a former clerk for Justice Sandra Day O'Connor. Currently, he sits on the board of the school he founded and is a clinical professor of law at Yale Law School. His scholarly interests are criminal, juvenile, and education law, particularly through the lens of race and class. Forman's work has been published in the *Yale Law Journal*, *UCLA Law Review*, *Michigan Law Review*, and *Georgetown Law Journal*, among others.

David Greenberg is the co-founder of El Colegio. He is a licensed social studies teacher who has worked at the school as an advisor, special education and lead teacher, and administrative and executive director. David has served on the board of directors of the EdVisions Cooperative and Minnesota Association of Charter Schools. He lives in Minneapolis with his wife and daughter, who recently started kindergarten in the Minneapolis Public Schools.

Marvin Hoffman is the founding director of University of Chicago Charter School North Kenwood/Oakland campus and currently the associate director of the University's Urban Teacher Education Program. He leads the program's Academic and Soul Strands of the Foundations of Education Sequence. Marv boasts an extensive teaching career that spans over 40 years and encompasses preschool through graduate school instruction. Prior to teaching in Chicago, Hoffman taught in numerous states, including Mississippi, New York, New Hampshire, Vermont, and Texas. He is the author of three books: *Vermont Diary*, *Chasing Hellhounds: A Teacher Learns from His Students*, and *You Won't Remember Me: The Schoolboys of Barbiana Speak to Today*. Marv received his Ph.D. in clinical psychology from Harvard University.

Dennis Littky is the co-founder of The Met School, Big Picture Learning, and College Unbound, and the author of *The Big Picture: Education is Everyone's Business*. He is also the subject of *A Town Torn Apart*, a made-for-TV movie starring *L.A. Law*'s Michael Tucker. Dennis has a Ph.D. in education and psychology and has received a Principal of the Year award and the McGraw-Hill Education Award for Excellence, and he is one of George Lucas's Daring Dozen in Education.

Rito Martinez is currently director of Leadership Development for the School Leadership Preparation Program and senior leadership coach with the Network for College Success at the University of Chicago's School of Social Service Administration. Mr. Martinez grew up in Little Village, and taught for 12 years at Morton East High School, where he won the prestigious Golden Apple Award for Excellence in Teaching. His extraordinary leadership and community development efforts as the founding principal of Social Justice High School earned him the Little Village Community Development Community Service Award. Rito lives in Oak Park with his wife and three sons.

Deborah W. Meier is the founder of Central Park East Secondary School, a New York City public high school in which more than 90% of the entering students went on to college, mostly to four-year schools. Currently, she is a senior scholar in New York University's Steinhardt School of Education as well as a board member and director of New Ventures at Mission Hill, director and advisor to Forum for Democracy and Education, and on the board of the Coalition of Essential Schools. Her books, *The Power of Their Ideas, Lessons to America from a Small School in Harlem* (1995), *Will Standards Save Public Education* (2000), *In Schools We Trust* (2002), *Keeping School*, with Ted and Nancy Sizer (2004) and *Many Children Left Behind* (2004) are all published by Beacon Press. Her most recent book, *Playing for Keeps*, written with Brenda Engel and Beth Taylor, is published by Teachers College Press.

Samuel Seidel is the author of the forthcoming book *Hip Hop Genius: Remixing High School Education* (Rowan & Littlefield, 2011), which offers a deep look at the High School for Recording Arts and contextualizes the school's work within the field of hip-hop education. Seidel has taught in a wide range of settings and directed youth programs. He currently speaks nationally on youth development strategies and serves as an education consultant. More of his writing can be found at the HusslingtonPost.com.

Phyllis Tashlik is currently director of the Center for Inquiry, the professional development center of the New York Performance Standards Consortium. A teacher for several decades in the New York City public schools, Tashlik has taught English and writing classes, helped begin small schools, developed literacy curricula, and published student writing. She is editor of *Active Voices II*; *Hispanic, Female and Young*; and a writer/director for Teacher to Teacher Publications.

Elliot Washor is co-founder and co-director of Big Picture Learning, and co-founder of The MET Center. Elliot has been involved in school reform for more than 35 years as a teacher, principal, administrator, producer, and writer. He is one of the George Lucas Education Foundation's Daring Dozen—The Twelve Most Daring Educators. Elliot lives in San Diego with his wife and five dogs.

Index